HOW TO WRITE

FICTION

AND

NON-FICTION

(Revised version)

Written
By
Nigel D. Salmon

Contents

How To Write Fiction

How To Write Non-fiction

How To Self Publish Your Book

How To Write Fiction

Introduction

Fiction is literary writing based on the imagination. The beauty about fiction is that it allows you to tell a world that exists in your own mind. You become the god of that world, deciding how places will look and the fate of the people operating in such places. As god of your imaginary world, you decide when the characters speak, sleep, fight, love, and who will die from who will live to the end.

Fiction does not start and end with your imagination. When you imagine a world and describe it, the reader will read your description and thus see the same world in her own mind. Apparently, your imagination is transferred into the mind of the reader through words.

Your tools as a writer are your words. Using descriptive words, you paint pictures in the mind of the reader and also evoke emotions. You can make the reader see a glum or cheery world. You can make the reader laugh, smile, or feel anger or pity. Found in your tools (words) are six most popular literary devices for bringing different effects on the reader. These devices are simile, metaphor, personification, onomatopoeia, hyperbole, and part of speech.

Simile

A simile is a phrase that compares one thing to another with use of the word 'as' or 'like.' Simile makes a description more cogent and interesting. Look at the example below:

I knelt on the floor and peered into the basement below. It was as dark as an underground tunnel.

The simile in the passage is 'as dark as an underground tunnel.' It makes the passage more interesting than to have simply written *it was dark* or *it was very dark.*

When using simile, the two things you compare must be different in kind. They cannot be the same. As seen in the example on the previous page, the dark basement is compared to a dark tunnel. A basement and a tunnel are different.

Metaphor

When a writer uses metaphor, he uses a word or phrase to suggest something different from their literal meaning. Look at the following example:

Fitz Jackson reclines in the chair and stares back at Jake with a heart of stone.

The metaphor in the passage is 'heart of stone'—which means that Fitz Jackson is feeling no compassion or love for Jake.
The following is an example of a one word metaphor:

"You dog," Miranda bluntly utters to her cheating boyfriend.

The word 'dog' is the metaphor. You may use metaphors anywhere in your story. Metaphors help make description more interesting.

It is important, though, that you do not use a lot of metaphors in a children story. A child, especially a child under age 10, might not properly fathom a story that has a lot of metaphors.

Personification

Personification is description which gives human characteristic to a non-human or non-living thing. It keeps a description from being too simple or dull to the reader. Look at the following example:

The wet pair of boots cries with a scrubbing sound with every hurried step she makes along the dark and slippery track.

The phrase pair of boots cries gives human quality to the shoes.

Onomatopoeia

Onomatopoeia is the use of words that sound like the things they refer to. It is important to use onomatopoeia in a story. The reader should know what sounds the things around a character make, especially in a scary scene.

Look at the following example:

The door squeaks open by Cindy's gentle but cautious push. Suddenly she hears a whoosh over her head from inside the rickety warehouse. Cindy throws her face over her shoulder and glimpses a bat flying out into the cold and stygian night.

The use of the words 'squeaks' and 'whoosh' is onomatopoeia.

It is easy to make a mistake with onomatopoeia. Apart from the very mistake of spelling the word, there is the mistake of applying the use of it. Remember, the word you use must sound like the thing it refers to. It would be incorrect to write, for example, the following:

The sizzling pot of porridge draws the attention of the hungry wolf.

Why is the above sentence incorrect? A pot of porridge does not give a 'sizzling' sound.

With onomatopoeia you may form your own word when there is none in your vocabulary (or a dictionary) to mimic a particular sound you have in mind. For example:

I was immediately distracted by the bapping sound of the crawling jalopy.

The word 'bapping' in the passage would be a writer-invented locution.

Hyperbole

Hyperbole is a way of speaking or writing that exaggerates things and is not meant to be taken literally. Why would a writer use hyperbole? The answer is to make a description more lucid and interesting. Look at the following example:

The livid donkey leaps in front the thief with glaring eyes and tunnel-wide nostrils.

The phrase *'tunnel-wide nostrils'* is hyperbole. It cannot be taken literally, but it gives the reader an intensified picture of the angry donkey.

Part Of Speech

Part of speech is one of the categories into which words can be divided—such as nouns, verbs, prepositions, etc. For descriptive writing, the two parts of speech you will use are adjectives and adverbs. You will use them to describe the nouns and verbs in your writing.

Using adjectives and adverbs, you will turn simple sentences into descriptive sentences so that you give more details to the reader. Look at the examples below.

Simple Sentence:

The boy walks toward the door.

The above sentence is simple because the nouns and the verb are not described. The reader gets no details about the nouns *boy* and *door* and no detail about the verb *walks*. So to put specific pictures in the mind of the reader, the nouns and the verb must be described using adjectives (for the nouns) and adverb (for the verb).

Descriptive Sentence:

The fat boy slowly walks toward the slab door.

Now you can see that by using the adjective **fat** to describe the boy, the reader now has a specific picture of the boy. By using the adverb **slowly** to describe the verb, the reader now has a specific picture of how the boy walks. The adjective **slab** gives the reader a specific picture of the door.

So as you can clearly see, these six devices—simile, metaphor, personification, onomatopoeia, hyperbole, and part of speech—are tools for descriptive writing. They embellish a story and thus serve to fascinate the reader. One excellent example for any writer is the famous and late writer, William Shakespeare (1564-1616). Readers are not fascinated by Shakespeare simply because he was a writer but because of his literary genre. This 15th century writer's art form encompasses poetic devices in such a manner unforgettable.

So let your writing encompasses these six devices to erase 'dull and boring' from your stories.

Increase Your Vocabulary

It is important as a writer that you always learn new words. You cannot be very descriptive when your vocabulary is weak. To show dexterity, you must move beyond the simple and banal use of words—such as she <u>asks</u>; he <u>replies</u>. The more words you know the better you will be at painting lucid pictures in the mind of the reader. To increase your vocabulary, you are encouraged to apply the following:

Read often: To be a better writer you first need to be a better reader. When you read often, you allow yourself to be familiar with new words and phrases. So read, read, and read. Not only will you learn new words and phrases, you will—as you read books by different authors—learn techniques which you may apply to your own writing.

Use alternative words: You should not stay within the day-to-day use of words in your writing. The use of alternative words will keep your story from being dull. For example, instead of writing *John says* over and over in the same passage, what about using alternative words like John utters, breathes; remarks? If you keep writing that John says, Sandy says, John says, Sandy says in a dialogue—the dialogue will be monotonous to the reader.

You will need to use words that show a character's emotion (example: snarl) a character's vocal volume (example: whisper, yell) and vocal speed (example: snap, drawl). So you should not only write that John says. It is better to use a word that shows <u>how</u> he says it—example: John barks.

Research: You must conduct a research when you do not have the right words in your vocabulary to describe a thing or place in your story. For example: Your story is set on the rule of an ancient, Roman emperor.   How will you describe the apparels of the Roman emperor? How will you describe ancient Rome—such as diurnal life and different elements of buildings?   Obviously, if your vocabulary does not contain the words and names to describe your story, you will need to do a research on the internet and even in books.

The advice here is not for you to write grandiloquent stories. Absolutely not! The point is that if your vocabulary is weak—generally or for a particular setting—your story will be weak. The more phrases, names and words you know, the better you will be writing interesting stories.

You may access alternative words by using a lexicon that is a thesaurus.

Start with short stories

As a new writer, it is best to start with the short story. It is not a recommended endeavour to attempt a novel in the beginning. Every writer will face some kind of a failure in his or her writing in the beginning. It is easy to re-write a story of 30 pages after a failure than to re-write a 400-page novel after months of writing.

There is no official word or page count between the novel and the short story. So at first sight persons tend to differentiate base on book size. This is a common way of spotting the difference, because a book is either too short to be a novel or too long to be a short story. So where does the boundary between the short story and the novel begin? It is hard to specifically answer. A fiction of 300 pages and another of 600 pages, for example, can both be novels. Usually, a book is published as a novel based on the decision of the publisher. So the publisher may publish a 290 pages book as a novel and publish another 290 pages book as a short story based on several factors.

What exactly is the short story? The word 'short' is the antonym (opposite) of long. So to say short story means that there is a long story. Such long story, of course, is the novel. So in definition, the short story is a narrative that is less (primarily in words) to the novel. It can be further defined as a story that can be entirely read in one sitting.

The structure of the short story may be broken down as follows:

1. **A simple plot.** The story uses a small cast of characters around one problem or moral lesson. The plot does not extend significantly outside the problem or moral lesson.

2. **Few words:** Because the story uses a simple plot, the writer concludes it early, thus leading to a book with not many words and pages plus a short reading time.

A novel gives more in contents to the reader and is typically made up of the two following components:

1. **A complex plot.** The story has the plot (main course of events) and extends outside this with minor courses of events along the storyline. There may even be more than one plot. The plot is more elaborate (containing more details and twists) as a means to stretch the story to achieve a late conclusion. Because it is an extended story, more characters are typically used.

2. **Many words:** Because the story uses a complex plot, the conclusion is not early, thus leading to a book with many words and pages plus a long reading time.

A novel should be attempted by an experienced writer, someone who has learnt from story-writing errors; who now knows the rules and can keep a long story interesting. You should not attempt a novel if you have not proven your writing ability with a short story— especially if you are a writer who does not self publishes your work. This is not to say that a writer's first story cannot be a novel.

Without first understanding story-writing rules, you may write a 500-page disjointed story and think you have written a novel, when your story is really 280 pages with 220 pages of useless details. Story-writing is a craft. You will have to learn it as you write. And as you write, you become better. Writing a story is like constructing a building. If a man does not know the rules of building a one bedroom house, how will he knowledgeably build a skyscraper?

So you are encouraged to shape and strengthen your writing ability by starting with the short story.

....

The first section of this book is to show you how to write fiction. Whether you will write children or adult stories, this is a recommended book for your learning.   This book should help you improve significantly on how you approach fiction writing. You will get a vivid understanding of laying the foundation of a story and writing it.

There are rules to writing fiction. How many of the rules do you know?

A story is like a building. For a building, the builder will first need to have a plan and then build on it from the ground, block upon block. For a story, the writer will first need to have an idea and then develop the plot, building on it scene upon scene. When you understand the rules, you become the architect and interior decorator of your story. You will satisfactorily complete everything. So when the reader comes, she can relax with a cup of coffee and enjoy your finished work.

The fact that you have read this far show that you have an interest to learn. With no need to elongate this introduction, you will now be taken into the lesson of how to write fiction.

Writing Your Story

Before going into writing a story, it is important to first analyze a story by looking at its <u>definition</u> and its <u>elements</u>. In definition, a story is 'a narrative description of chained events which as a whole teach a lesson or inform about something or someone.' The purpose of a story is to entertain or educate, or the combination of both.

The major elements of a story (called 'literary elements') are plot, setting, mood, and characters.

Plot: The main sequence of the story.
Setting: The main time and place given to the story.
Mood: The main feeling or atmosphere created by the story.
Characters: Persons, animals or personified things used with or without dialogue in portraying the story.

<u>How To Start Writing</u>

The first step in writing a story is to come up with the <u>story idea</u>. The story idea is just a thought. For example, you might think "I want to write a story about a haunted house." This would be the story idea. Forming the story idea is the first important step. But this is not the time for you to start writing the story. If you start to write only on the story idea, you will face a lot of hiccups in your writing. Why? An idea is vague. It would be like going to a place without a map of where you are going. You will need a map.

And your map is a plot.

Plot

In definition, the plot is the main sequence of the story. So to write a story, you should first develop a description of it—called the 'plot description.' The plot description should be short and without details—such as names, dialogues, and description of places and things. Leave all of these for the story itself.

You should develop the plot description around the conflict you have in mind for the story. The conflict is an essential part of the plot. (If your story will not have a conflict, you should develop the plot description around <u>the lesson</u> your story will teach).

Look at the following example of a plot description:

Five college friends lodged at an old woman's house. One night they stole the old woman's gold necklace. They sold it and shared the money among themselves. After missing her necklace, the old woman revealed that the necklace has a curse and that whoever had stolen it will die within six days. A day later one of the five college friends died, shriveled to death inside the bathroom. Now the four remaining college friends must find the necklace and return it to avoid suffering the same effect of the curse. After trying to track down the buyer of the necklace without success, they decided to convince the old woman to halt the curse, only to find out that the old woman had died peacefully the night before in her sleep. Now desperate with only four days remained, the four college friends were thrown in a plight. Did they survive?

As you can see, the above plot description is short and without details. It also does not tell how the story ends. Yes, you should not decide (before you write) on how your story will end. You may have an idea for the ending but do not cement it into the plot description. By leaving the ending of the story free, you leave your creative mind open to fresh ideas that will come along while you write.

A plot may be imaginary—like the one in the example above—or based on a true story.

If you based your plot on a true story, your plot will follow the major sequence of the true story. The extent to which you will base your story on the true story will depend on you. Will you use the same names of persons from the true story? Will you use the same setting (time and place) from the true story? You will need to make your decision.

Genre

Genre (in terms of literature) is a category to which a story belongs. Genres may be decided by content, tone, method, or length. Genre should not be confused with other categories by which books are identified. For example, genre does not include categories such as dictionaries and encyclopaedias.

The purpose of genres is to separate compositions into individual groups that identify and serve particular interests. Relying on genres, booksellers can easily shelf books and readers easily find the ones of their interests.

Fiction has two main divisions, which are:

(a) Novels

(b) Short stories

Within these two main divisions the genres are many and include Comedy, Romance, Mystery, Tragicomedy, Action-Adventure, Fantasy, Gay, Séance fiction, and Horror.

The following is a look into some of the genres:

Action-Adventure

A story falls into this category because of the plot and the way the story is written. First the story must be set on an <u>adventure</u>. Example: The hero must go into a dangerous city in the Middle East to remove the hidden diary of an American nuclear scientist. This would be the adventure. Second the story must show <u>intense action</u> between opposing characters—example: physical fighting, shooting, car chase, etc. The story must also be suspenseful.

Put the two elements together (adventure plus actions) and you will have Action-adventure.

Romance

Romance is a love-story. In order for your story to be a romance, the plot must be centered on romantic love between two characters. The story must also be written using a romantic tone and mood.

The story must contain a third party (something, a group, or someone) that is the obstacle between the two characters in love.

Something: This may be distance, memory lost by one lover, imprisonment of one lover, diffidence, etc.

Group: This may be the family of one of the lovers, a homophobic community, a tribe, etc.

Someone: This is a person trying to keep apart the two lovers. Example, it is an undesirable woman trying to snare the protagonist and keep him apart from the damsel he truly loves.

The third party creates an obstacle and causes the conflict (the struggle for the two lovers to be together) in the story. Although it is a love-story, a romance may contain scenes of intense action (example: physical fights) and even tragedy.

People read romance to be inspired by a struggle for romantic love. The most interesting part is what happens to the two lovers in the end. This is where you have to be careful as the writer that you do not disappoint the reader. A romance has to have an admirably satisfying ending. The reader should be thinking "ah, that's so romantic" as she reads the closing scene of the story.

Never end a romance showing the two lovers defeated by their obstacle. They're hampered in many ways by it but not defeated by it.

To end a romance you must first bring the obstacle between the two lovers to an end. The end of their obstacle is the beginning of them living happily ever after. Well, 'living happily ever after' may not be what you have in mind for the end. It was certainly not what William Shakespeare had in mind when he wrote *Romeo and Juliet* who eventually committed suicide to be together. Anyway, your story must show to the reader two characters that went the ultimate against their obstacle and finally (in death or life) be together.

Mystery

For your story to be a mystery, it must be dealing with a puzzling crime. The crime is typically a murder, but the writer may choose something else to make the mystery—example: the disappearance of a priceless artifact or disappearance of someone. Uncertainty is the centre of a mystery. You will create the uncertainty by disguising mainly the motive and villain until near the end of the story.

The mystery may be set on one act of crime by the villain (example: a murder) or a series of crimes of the same nature (example: serial killer). Also, the villain may turn out to be not just one individual but a group of conspirators.

The hero in a mystery must be the character who is investigating the crime. You should not write a mystery in which the hero is not the one investigating the crime. But the hero does not have to be a police detective. Too many mysteries have been written casting the hero as a detective. The hero may be a character that has no training or experience in crime investigation but is a person driven by a strong desire to get to the truth about what had actually happened. For example: Your story is about the murder of a hotel manager. You may show a detective leading an investigation in the murder, but you center the story on the 16 years old niece of the late hotel manager who is stubbornly conducting her own investigation by herself. And it is her investigation—after personal risks and acts of stubbornness—which solves the mystery.

Creating the hero as a character with no training or experience in crime investigation (as you are) makes it easy for you to write the story. This is because you can portray the hero with the same limited knowledge that you have.   But if you create your hero as a police detective, you might not have enough researched knowledge about police detective work to suitably put your hero into action.

The crime in a mystery must be puzzling for the hero. You must lead the hero on dead-end trails, letting him think he knows when he doesn't. You must create suspicion over one or few characters to cause the reader to draw on wrong conclusions about who committed the crime. For the reader and the hero, the crime is a puzzle.

You will keep the hero and the reader curious to know when, where, who, how, and why. It is common to see a mystery unravel to the reader in the following order:

<u>Where:</u> location of the crime.

<u>When:</u> The exact time the crime had occurred.

<u>How:</u> Method used by the culprit.

<u>Who:</u> Identity of culprit revealed

<u>Why:</u> Motive.

Bringing a mystery to the end may be done in any of the two following ways:

<u>Unveil the villain through the hero:</u> In this approach, you let the reader know the identity of the villain only   when the hero knows. This means that the reader does not know more than the hero. Because you have the reader depending on the hero to know the answers to the mystery,   your story must show to the reader how the hero thinks and how he comes to his conclusion.   So do not only write that the hero is shadowing Mr. Domes.   Instead show the reader why the hero decides to shadow Mr. Domes. This puts the reader into the mind of the hero.

<u>Unveil the villain to the reader first:</u>   In this approach, you let the reader know the identity of the villain before the hero does. This way the reader sees potential dangers that the hero does not see and worries for the hero's safety. However, you cannot do this when writing from the 'first person point of view.' (You will learn about points of view on page 23).

The villain should not be a new character that you create near the end of the story. The villain must turn out to be a character that was always there—a character that the reader was not made to feel suspicious of. Also, importantly, you must identify which character you will reveal as the villain while you write the story. For example: Your mystery is set on a murder at an artiste management company. By identifying the secretary as the culprit before you start to write, you will find it easy to carefully position her through the story so that when she is revealed her <u>method</u> (how she possibly   committed the crime) and her <u>motive</u> are logically explained to the reader. So it is not a wise idea to, as you bring the story to a close, randomly choose one of the characters and say to the reader 'this is the culprit.'

The solving of the mystery is the conclusion of the story. So it might not be useful to add another chapter after the mystery is solved.

Gay

The gay genre covers stories of homosexual interests. For your story to fall into this genre, it must be written either with a homosexual theme or centered favourably on homosexuality. Stories in this genre typically focus on romantic attraction or relationship between characters. When this is not the case, the stories deal with common internal or external misconception or struggles of homosexuality.

Internal: A character, usually the protagonist, struggles with his or her homosexual feelings, either to understand it or how to express it.

External: Someone or a group creates a difficult situation for the protagonist because of his homosexuality. Example: He struggles for acceptance from most players on his college football team.

Comedy

For your story to be a comedy, the story must be written humorously by having a:

Comical tone (the manner in which you write the story)

Comical mood (generally humorous feeling created by the story)

Comical characters (but do not make all the characters comical because this might be overdoing it).

The humour must begin from the plot description. If you do not develop the plot with a sense of humour, you will likely fail to amuse the reader.

When thinking of writing a comedy, avoid subjects that are too sensitive or serious. (Example: The story is about a woman who was raped and now sets out to get justice). Not many readers will find anything humorous about a woman been raped. Instead you should choose a subject that is not indelicate or insensitive for the plot.

Settings

Setting establishes the time and place of occurrence. There are actually two settings in a story. There is the <u>major setting</u> and the <u>minor settings</u>.

Minor Settings

A minor setting establishes the time and place of a scene. For example: You write a scene with John Brown chasing Sam. Regarding **time,** is John Brown chasing Sam at midday, early morning, or late in the night? Regarding **place**, is the chase occurring along a highway, a crowded street, or along Duke Street in Kingston, Jamaica? The time and place you give to this scene is the setting—called 'minor setting' because it is different from the major setting of the story.

You must give a **mood** to every scene. So when establishing the time and place, you should also establish the mood. An example of a mood is 'dejected.' A mood may flow across multiple scenes base on what you are writing in the story. For example: Scene 1 shows old Mr. Blake lying gravely ill in bed and his wife sitting fretfully by his bedside, Scene 2 shows Mr. Blake's eldest son outside the house listening to the family doctor saying that the old man may not live for much longer, and Scene 3 shows Mr. Blake's youngest children sitting and conversing worriedly in the living room. All these three scenes carry the 'dejected' mood.

You will establish the mood through your tone (the way you write the scene) and the action of the character (how he appears, speaks and behaves).

It is important that the mood you give each scene plays well into the sequence of the plot.

Major Setting

The major setting establishes the time and place of the story itself. Regarding **time**, is the story set in the past, present, or future? Regarding **place**, is the story set in an imaginary place or real place? Let us take a closer look at both, starting with time:

Time

The Past: If you set your story in the past, the names of characters, what they wear,   the places they operate in, and the use of dialogues must fit the chosen time. For example: If you set your story in 17th century England, the characters must wear clothes typical in that time, speak in the language of that era, and be without the inventions of the present.

If your 17th century character is using a cell phone, for example, your story has the error called anachronism.

The Present: If you set your story in the present, the characters operate with some of the inventions of today—cell phones, internet, planes, etc. They will also utilize slangs and clothes of current time.

The Future: If you set your story in the future, you will write a science fiction. For your story to be set in the future, you must put your characters in a world (which is still Earth) where there are scientific advances beyond the present. Such scientific advances may include, for example, flying motorbikes.

Your story will not be set in the future by simply writing that the characters are living in the future. What is the future? The future is, as mentioned before, a world with scientific advances beyond the present. Such world must still be Earth otherwise your story will fall in the genre of fantasy.

Place

Now let us look at the second element in the major setting—which is 'place.'

Real Place: You will set your story in a real place by telling it in a place that actually exists—example: Cuba.

If you set your story on a real place, you must first know how the place looks and general things that happen there. This is important to ensure that a description you give is not incorrect. For example: If you set your story in New Delhi, India, do you know how people there generally dress? How do buildings there generally look?

When you set your story in a real place, you cannot logically include a thing that is not actually at the place. You cannot, for example, put characters on a beach when there is no beach at the place. If you do not understand a place, do not put your characters there. If you do, you must not attempt to give details you do not have.

Imaginary Place: You may tell your story in a place that is completely made-up. That is, a place that does not actually exist. You will invent the appearance of streets, buildings, etc. But even with an imaginary place, the layout has to make sense to the reader. For example, you cannot write that as Cindy jogs along the crowded street in the city, she waves to Peter in the middle of the forest. Such layout would appear rather silly. While the place is imaginary, it has to make sense to real life—except when you are writing a fantasy, which portrays a magical world in which pretty much anything goes.

The major setting must also have a **mood**, which will be the general mood of the story itself. Yes, the mood of the major setting is the mood of the story.

Though your story will contain scenes with different moods, you will not divagate from the general mood of the story. For example: When writing a romance, the fact that you write a dejected scene, angry scene, and frightful scene does not change the romantic mood—because the romantic mood dominates the story.

Quick Reminder:
There are two settings in a story: the major setting and minor settings.
Major setting establishes the time and place of the story itself. A minor setting establishes the time and place of a scene.

Points of View

You must choose a point of view from which to write your story. You may choose to write your story from the first person point of view, second person point of view, or third person point of view.

First person point of view

The term 'first person' means self. So to write a story from the *first person point of view* means that you will write the story from the point of view of self. You will write using first person singular (I, me, my, myself, mine) and first person plural (us, we, our, ourselves). You will notice as you write that the 'I' is conspicuous of all the pronouns. So choosing to write your story from the *first person point of view* is regarded as using the 'I' character. You will write the entire story through the senses of the 'I' character—what I see, I hear, I think, I taste, I smell, and I feel. The 'I' character is inevitably the central character.

The 'I' character may be given a name. But do not attempt to use such name to replace the 'I,' because this would throw the entire writing into the third person point of view. If you choose to give the 'I' character a name (using a proper noun), you may do so as follows:

*(a) **Direct Narration:*** Through this method, you tell the reader your own name. Look at the following example:

I am Pat Simpson, the 2010 Miss Canada Beauty Queen. I had a remarkably beautiful face and life until an unexpected tragedy took it all on a dark and rainy Friday night.

As you can see, the writer directly tells the reader her name. Now let us look at the other option.

(b) *A Character Calls The Name:* Through this method, the reader is told the name of the 'I' character through another character in the story. Look at the following example:

I hurried up the steps to the second floor at my high school, sweating and tired. Under ten seconds I was at the door to my classroom and noticed that all the other students were already seated. Panting but pretending relaxed, I stepped across the threshold into the quiet classroom with obvious trepidation.

"You are late again, Pamela," the teacher said, looking sternly over the frame of her spectacles at me.

As you can see, the reader is told the name of the 'I' character through another character in the story.

You are considered a *participant* in a story when you write from the *first person point of view*—though you might not be referring to your real self. The *first person point of view* is highly recommended for writing autobiography and memoirs. When using it for fiction, here are some very important tips:

You must not have a scene in your story where the 'I" character is not present. The 'I' character has to be in every scene of the story. Also, anything outside the knowledge of the 'I' character cannot be described. Look at the following example with this error:

Here I sit in the kitchen, sipping from a cup of black coffee while my husband is at this time locked inside the bedroom with that young helper. They are naked in bed. He is massaging her bare breasts while playing his long tongue against her ear.....**Incorrect!**

In order for the 'I' character to know that her husband is massaging the helper's breasts and playing his tongue against her ear, the 'I' character would have to be there—inside the bedroom—and witnessing such acts.   The 'I' character cannot describe what is happening outside his (or her) presence.

Also, only the thoughts of the 'I' character can be described. You must not attempt to describe   the thoughts of any other character in the story. The other characters would have to describe their thoughts, in the presence of the 'I' character, for their thoughts to be described.

Look at this error in the following example:

I look across the desk at Jack. He sits in front me with a worried countenance, thinking deeply about his financial problems ....**Incorrect!**

At no time can the "I" character describe the thought of another character. But what you can do is to write that the 'I' character is assuming. Look at the same example without the error:

I look across the desk at Jack. He sits in front me with a worried countenance, giving me the impression he is thinking deeply about his financial problems.

As you can clearly see, the *first person point of view* puts limitation on the writer. But like many writers, you may write a successful story from this point of view.

Second person point of view

The term 'second person' means the person being spoken to or written to. A piece of writing using the *second person point of view* makes its audience subject of attention for the writer. So choosing to write from the *second person point of view* means that you will include the reader in what you write by use of the references 'your,' 'yours,' 'yourself,' and 'you.' An example of a work using the *second person point of view* is this very book. You might have already noticed that this book is written from the *second person point of view*. The reader of this literature is included in the book as the second person by being addressed as 'you.'

The *second person point of view* is used by every writer when writing monologues and dialogues. Example: *"Who are you?" Cindy asks.* But many writers avoid using the *second person point of view* to tell an entire story. This is because using 'you' and 'your,' the *second person point of view* creates the 'you' character—which is not popular in fiction.

Though unpopular and rarely used in fiction writing, nothing is disastrously wrong with the 'you' character. This is a character that can even be used as the central character in a story. Look at the following example of this:

It is 6pm Friday evening. All the other employees have left, fortunately leaving you alone with Julia in the work room. You are sitting at your desk and realizing that this is now your chance to let her know how you are attracted to her. With your blue eyes observing her, it is clear to your mind that she is finishing up on a last document at her desk before leaving. The scribbling motion of her right hand with the red pen hints that she will take steps from her desk within few minutes. You know that you have only limited time to act.

In the silence of the work room, you rise from your desk. With all the other employees out of the room, you feel a boldness to express your emotion as you approach her desk, losing that nervousness you held for the last two weeks since you first met her. "Need help finishing up that document?" You ask, smiling at her.

"Actually, no," Julia replies. "I'm done."

So as you can see, the 'you' character is not difficult to use in the portrayal of a story. Note that if you decide to use the 'you' character, you must not have a scene in your story where the 'you" character is not present. The 'you' character has to be in every scene of the story. Also, anything outside the knowledge of the 'you' character cannot be described.

The 'you' character is popular to some extent in children fiction, though not as the protagonist. In a children story, you can use the *second person point of view* to take the child reader on an adventure. You may write, for example: *Did you see the green snake in the tree? No? It must be somewhere else.*

Third person point of view

The term 'third person' means a party other than 'I' or 'you.' In other words, it is a party that is not considered the writer or reader. If you choose to write from the *third person point of view*, you will use third person singular and plural when referring to the characters — such as he, she, it, their, etc.

On next page, look at the following example:

David strolls to the balcony. He looks with a yawn at the white-sand beach below.

Does 'he' in the example refer to me, you, or a third person? It refers to the third person. So David is not me or you. David is obviously the third person.

The *third person point of view* throws the reader into the position of *observer*. This is because the reader's presence cannot be felt in the story. The writer's presence, though, is felt as the narrator.

Though this is the most popular and favourite point of view among authors, the *third person point of view* should not be used when writing an autobiography or any personal account.

This point of view allows you to be omniscient. It actually puts no limitation on a writer. With the *third person point of view*, you can tell the reader what is going on anywhere in the story. You can reveal potential dangers to the reader before characters in the story see them. You can easily make any of the characters in the story the central character, and you can easily describe the thoughts of any character in the story. The *third person point of view* allows you to be omniscient in how you share information to the reader.

However, this does not mean that you should make your story predictable. While the *third person point of view* allows you to describe anything, anywhere in your story, you must follow the big rule of hiding information from the reader to keep the reader curious.

Remember, if the reader can predict the outcome of your story, there is awfully no reason for her to continue reading it. As all successful authors know, a good story is a story with a surprising element or twist near the ending. In fact, several twists along the plot will do better.

So, does the *third person point of view* sound best to you? Or do you prefer the second person or first person point of view? The particular point of view you choose may rest with the type of story you will write or what best works for you.

Choosing the tense for your story

You must choose to write your story using either the past tense or present tense. Examples of tense: come (present tense), came (past tense), will come (future tense).

Past Tense

If you wish to write your story in the past tense, all verbs in your story must show past occurrences. Example: It <u>was</u> midnight. David <u>had</u> already <u>hid</u> himself between the two huge flower pots on Olivia's verandah. Quietly he <u>approached</u> her window while she <u>slept</u>.

There are only two exceptions for switching from the past tense. These exceptions are:

(a) *When writing a direct speech in a dialogue.* Example: "I feel the same way about you," Lucy said. (A verb in direct speech or quote does not change tense).

(b) *When describing a future action.* Example: Dave sat on the big stone at the foot of the hill. It was obvious that he would have <u>to climb</u> it alone to the very top.

Present Tense

If you will use the present tense, all verbs in your story will show actions happening now. Example: It <u>is</u> midnight. David <u>is</u> <u>hiding</u> between the two huge flower pots on Olivia's verandah. Quietly he <u>approaches</u> her window while she <u>sleeps.</u>

When using the present tense to write your story, the past tense is used but only when showing previous actions. Example: As David stands at the window, he   remembers that he had <u>left</u> the missing glove in the garden while he <u>was</u> there. The use of the past tense 'left' and 'was' is necessary because they show previous actions.

There is also room for use of the future tense. Example: David stands at the window, pondering how he <u>will enter</u> her room. The use of 'will enter' puts the action of the character in the future.

Future tense

The future tense is made up of two verbs—an auxiliary verb and an action verb. Example: *He will fix my broken computer tonight. Or I want to tell him the truth.*

It might not be judicious to write an entire story using the future tense. Example: *It will be midnight. David will hide between the two huge flower pots on Olivia's verandah. He will come to her window while she will sleep.*

If your intention is to set your story in the future, you will not accomplish this through use of the future tense. Tense (past, present, or future) shows time of occurrences in the story—not the time of the story itself. The time of the story is typically shown through the setting (see 'Settings' on page 20). This is why you may set your story in the 1930s (the past) but write it using the present tense.

Summary

Plot: What is your story mainly about?

Genre: Apart from being a novel or short story, do you want to write a comedy, romance, action-adventure, etc?

Setting: Will your story be set in the past, present or future? Will it be set on an imaginary place or a real place? If set on a real place, what can you tell the reader about that place?

Points of View: Will you write the story from the first person, second person, or third person point of view?

Past tense or present tense: Will you tell the story in the past tense or present tense? You cannot choose both. (If you set your story in the future, it would be better to tell it in the present tense).

The Conflict

In definition, the conflict of a story is the struggle (or main struggle) in the story. You will introduce the conflict in the story through two steps—complication and reaction.

Complication: This is the event or events that create the problem for the protagonist. Example: A group of barbarians are coming to attack his city.

Reaction: This is the point from which the protagonist decides to take action against the problem. But do not simply show your protagonist (or hero) reacting. To show your hero reacting against the problem, you must first give him a motive. The problem facing him is not his motive. Remember, many individuals when faced with a problem decide to surrender, run or do nothing. Since your hero will challenge the problem, you must show his motive (reason) for choosing to do so. Example: He is patriotic and brave, and this is why he remains to fight the coming barbarians. With the protagonist reacting against the problem, your story now has the conflict.

You may introduce the conflict by showing the reaction before the complication. In other words, you show the protagonist reacting to the problem before you show the reader exactly what the problem is and how it began. Demonstration of this can be seen in many books and films. Example: The movie starts by showing the hero parachuting into a forest with guns and military gears. Down in the forest he is seen cautiously moving along. You are sitting there watching the movie without any glue of why the hero has decided to enter the forest. But as you watch, maybe ten minutes late, you learn that the hero is trying to find a kidnapped spy agent.

The kidnapping incident is the Complication, and the rescue mission is the Reaction. But the movie shows the rescue mission first.
If you write the conflict showing the reaction first, you are playing around the order of logics. Can a man react to pain without first feeling it? Within the order of logics, reaction comes after, not first. So when you show reaction first, much caution is required to give your story a logical sequence. And how do you do that?

When you show reaction before complication, you will bring back the order of logics to the conflict by using the literary device called backstory. Backstory, in definition, is a past story or past events that add meaning to or explain current circumstances. Using backstory, you will show the complication either through *flashback* (character thinks back on the events which created the problem), *dialogues* (characters discussed the events that created the problem), or *exposition* (writer explains to the reader directly). This way the reader at the end of the story sees the complication as happening before the reaction.

When a story is written with a conflict, the conflict typically becomes the focus of the story and is the thing which mostly holds the interest of the reader to the story. There are two types of conflicts:

(a) Internal conflict.
(b) External conflict.

Internal conflict

An internal conflict occurs in either the body or mind. Physically, it may be a disease—example: Parkinson's disease. Psychologically, it may be something such as depression. Whatever it is, the character will struggle against self. He will struggle to overcome (or come to acceptance with) his physical or psychological problem.

External conflict

An external conflict occurs outside the body or mind. It may be set on any of the following:

Character against character: In this type of external conflict, you will put one character against another—typically, hero against villain. The conflict of the story is the two characters against each other. For example: The hero competing against the villain for a young woman.

Person against group: In this type of external conflict, one character is against a group of characters—example: a black man against a racist neighbourhood.

Person against thing: In this type of external conflict, you will put a human character against something that is not human. The thing may be an animal, ghost, alien creature, etc.

Nature of a conflict

The way you write the conflict of a story will determine whether it is a violent or mild conflict. Let us take a closer look at both.

Violent Conflict

This is a conflict that is characterized by violence. The conflict of the story is fought violently between characters and may include the use of weapons. Details are graphic and dialogues may be explicit.

Not all stories are suitable for a violent conflict, base on the intended readers (example: children) and the intended genre. Regarding genres, romance and comedy, just to name two, should not use a violent conflict. You should not attempt to write the conflict of these stories in violence. This is because romance is set on love—not violence, though there can be scenes of physical fighting or tragedy. Comedy is set on amusement—not violence. On the other hand, the genres that may be written with a violent conflict include action-adventure, mystery, and horror.

Mild Conflict

This is a conflict which contains no violence. If it contains violence, the violence is not explicit or graphic and omits details that would be horrifying. A mild conflict should be used in a children story and also should be used in a romance and comedy.

Enlivening the conflict

For your story to be interesting, the solving of the conflict must be delayed by   unfortunate coincidences put in the way of the hero.

Without unfortunate coincidences, the conflict would fail to be a real conflict and you would thus have an uninteresting story. For example: Your story is about David who wants to eliminate a haunting ghost from the house he bought. He phones an exorcist who then comes over and gets rid of the ghost. Where is the real conflict in that?

For the conflict to be interesting, you will need to create unfortunate coincidences in David's way. So you may write that David calls in the exorcist to get rid of the haunting ghost from his house. When the exorcist comes over, the ghost throws a lamp at him, causing him to move backwards, falls through a window of the house and dies. David still has the problem of the haunting ghost. You will write that David tries again to eliminate the ghost and fails; he tries and fails, he tries and fails—each failure caused by an unfortunate coincidence. Eventually, by learning from the failures, David succeeds in his struggle to eliminate the ghost.

The small unfortunate coincidences zigzag the conflict (David's struggle to eliminate the haunting ghost) and create a struggle that interests the reader.

If your story is dealing with an internal conflict, you will zigzag it by showing the character overcoming his problem then fails, almost overcome and fails, until he finally succeeds by coming to acceptance of his problem (example: HIV) or eliminate his problem (example: anorexia).

Each small difficulty (unfortunate coincidence) must fit into a scene well, and they must work against the hero and in favour of the villain. For example: The hero is chasing the villain across the street; then a moving bus comes in the way of the hero and causes the villain to escape on his merry way. That is an unfortunate coincidence that works!

Apart from making the story interesting, each unfortunate coincidence must help push the plot toward its climax by either making the hero more determined, wise, courageous, less forgiving, or something else. Yes, the unfortunate coincidences must (apart from zigzagging and slowing down the solving of the conflict) affect some kind of change in the hero.

Unsolved conflict

In some stories, the conflict was never solved. Such stories are typically written to teach a lesson or to inspire. For example, you may write a story about a woman's struggle against breast cancer. The conflict of the story is the woman's struggle against the breast cancer. Eventually, the woman (protagonist) dies from the cancer. This would be a story with an unsolved conflict (a conflict is considered 'solved' if the hero wins). But, importantly, your story serves to inspire women living with breast cancer in real life to be strong like the woman in your story or teach the lesson that ignoring early testing might lead to death.

A story in which the conflict was never solved (but should show corollary) can teach a very useful lesson—such as 'illegal drugs will kill you.' If a short story is all about teaching a moral lesson, it is called an allegory.

Another reason for the unsolved conflict is when the author sets the story on a real life crime that is unsolved.

Start the conflict early

If you do not start your story with the conflict, it is important that you start the conflict early in the story. The conflict typically takes the focus of the story.

The longer you take to get to the conflict, the less the reader will care about the things (setting, characters, etc) that you keep describing. So you should not bore the reader with exposition. The earlier you get to the conflict, the more likely it is that the reader will continue reading.

Character Development

You will create characters to carry out your story. You obviously cannot have a story without them. A character is a person, animal or personified thing used with or without dialogue in portraying a story. But this book will deal only with human characters.

Purpose of characters

The first rule about character development is that each character must have a purpose. You must never create a character that does not contribute to your story. Is a character part of the plot or part of the background in a scene? You must decide.

Feature and minor characters

In a story, there are the feature characters and minor characters. Feature characters are the characters that are important to the plot. You use them repeatedly in the execution of the plot. You must give the reader a thorough description of them. Minor characters, on the other hand, are characters that are not important to the plot, such as background characters.

....

You will create a character by describing a person to the reader. Unless you are hiding the identity of a character (such as in a mystery where a character may only be known as 'the killer' until exposed), the reader must first know whether a character is male or female. The reader must know what each character looks like. So when describing your characters to the reader, you are to apply the following:

The physical appearance of a character

Apart from the reader knowing that the character is male or female, is the person fat or slim? Is the person tall or short? What are the

colour and the length of the person's hair?

Naming your characters

You will name your characters using proper nouns or common nouns, or the combination of both in your story.

A *proper noun* is a specific name that identifies someone or something outside of a class—examples: Peter, David, Harry Potter. So if you identify a character with a specific name such as 'David,' you are using a proper noun.

A *common noun* means any or all members of a class—example: witch, man, prince, boy. So if you identify a character as 'the Witch' through the story, you are using a common noun. An unnamed character is one identified only by a common noun. You may write an entire story identifying your characters using only common nouns. But this is recommended only for a very short story.

Remember to be consistent when using a common noun to identify a character. What does it mean to be consistent? If you identify a character as 'the Damsel,' for example, you must consistently identify her that way through the story. Also, the common noun which is used with a definite article should begin with a capital letter—example: the Damsel, instead of 'the damsel."

Clothes, movement and emotion of the characters

The reader needs to know what each character is **wearing**, **doing**, and **feeling** in a scene. A scene will be dull if you leave these out. Let us look at these three things:

Clothes: You must dress your characters in each scene. The clothes you put on a character must fit the scene and even the personality of the character. Regarding scene, how would you dress a character in a courtroom? Regarding personality, how would you dress a character that is a street gangster?

There are other things you should take into consideration when dressing your characters. If your character is a poor and homeless man, how will you dress him? How would you dress a catholic priest? How would you dress a female prostitute working at a street corner in the night? You cannot put any clothes on any character. You will have to dress to fit.

Clothes are important. When you fail to dress a character, you fail to let the reader fully see the character.

Action: You must describe the action of each character in a scene. Some writers tend to stop describing the actions of the characters in a dialogue. This puts the reader out of the scene, letting the reader feels as if she is standing outside the locked door of a room and listening to a conversation from the inside.

You will need to put the reader inside the room. The reader needs to see what the characters are doing as they talk. The reader needs to know that John Dickson is fondling a red pen and reclines in his office chair as he asks Kevin a question. The reader needs to know that Kevin crosses his legs as he replies to John Dickson's question. You will need to give action to your characters during dialogues. Some simple things like a character scratches his chin, takes in a deep breath, combs his fingers through his hair, raises an eyebrow, etc. bring life to a dialogue in a scene.

Emotions: You must give emotions to your characters. The reader needs to know when a character is happy, sad, disgusted, angry, and so on. You must not write a story in which you do not give emotions to your characters.

But do not just always tell the reader that a character is angry, sad, etc. Instead, you should show the reader. If you want to tell the reader that John is angry, you could describe John huffing with clenched fists and even kicking over a table. This is better than just writing that John is angry. The use of action to describe an emotion makes the emotion much clearer.

The Hero

The first character we will be looking at is the hero. The hero is the central character that the reader depends on to solve the conflict.

A hero only exists when the story is written with a conflict to be solved. So if there is no conflict in your story; there is no hero.   The absence of a hero, though, does not mean the absence of a <u>central character</u>. In the famous allegory *The Boy Who Cried Wolf*, there is no conflict and so there is no hero. But the central character in the story is 'the Boy.' A central character is only a hero when the story has a conflict showing that central character confronting it and later solving it.

The hero in your story must be thoroughly described. The reader must know his personality; his interests; his race, and his facial and physical appearance. If you will name your characters (meaning you identify them using proper nouns), the reader must also know the hero's name. The hero's name is important and must be chosen to fit him well.

Also, does your hero have a peculiar way of speaking? Example: lisping. Does he have a quirk or habit? Example: Smoking. What are his strength and his weakness in dealing with the conflict? Example: He cannot fight but is very smart. What will interest the reader most about your hero? Example: his eccentricity or his psychic power.

The point is that your hero should not be vague to the reader.

When giving the description of your hero, you must not put all the information into one paragraph or chapter. You will, as you write the story, release pieces of information about him. However, some information must come out in the beginning. These are the hero's gender, race, age (or age group—example: in his twenties), and his name.

Putting the hero in action

To put your hero in action you must give him a motive. For example: He is framed for a murder and he must prove his innocence. Been framed is his problem. To prove his innocence is the motive for action. So you should let the reader clearly understand the hero's reason to act.

It is important that you justify every harmful or deadly action of your hero. If you show your hero punching someone in the face, the question of why he is doing it must be seen by the reader. Even if your hero is a member of a street gang, hardened by the streets, failure to justify the actions of the hero is failure to show the reader a hero. Why so?   In a story, the hero has to be the character whose actions are justifiable; otherwise the reader will see him as a villain. If your story is dealing with an internal conflict, you must first show the effects of the psychological or physical problem before you put the hero into action against it.

Strength of the hero

Your hero must have a particular strength for dealing with the conflict. It does not have to be physical strength. The idea that the hero has to be someone who is physically strong and always takes on physical risks is misleading. Your hero's strength does not have to be physical.   Instead, your hero may be a physical coward whose strength for dealing with the conflict is being smart. Apart from physical strength, the strength of a hero may be his being perceptive, ambitious, psychic or stubborn in a particular belief.

It is best to bring out the hero's strength base on how the conflict (main problem) of the story affects him. So for example, your hero is a high school student who is regularly bullied by another student (the villain) at school. The villain verbally and physically harasses your hero every day. Your hero is a physical coward; so you write that a third character encourages him to take karate lessons to defend himself. (At this point the reader is made to think that the hero will find the physical strength to beat down the villain, but there is a twist).   The hero finishes his karate lessons and now can defend himself.   As he is walking home from school one evening, the villain attacks him, slapping him on the head and harassing him. Now a man attacks the villain.

"Give me the money you owe me!" the man shouts to the villain, grabbing him by his shirt collar and shoving him against a wall.

The high school student (villain) is unable to beat the man and does not have any money to pay the man.   So the man decides to stab him to death. Your hero, seeing what is about to happen, draws for his karate skills and kicks down the man, takes away his knife and causes the man to run away in fear. The villain after seeing how the hero has saved his life decides never to bully him again, and both become friends.

The hero's strength in this story is not his karate skills. The reader is led to expect this to be the hero's strength for dealing with his problem.   But the hero's strength is the very thing he has possessed all along—his 'kindness.' By showing kindness to the villain (saving his life) he ends the conflict of the story.

Note: When you bring out your hero's strength, ensure that the transition primarily changes how the hero reacts to his problem instead of who he is.

Series hero

If you are writing a series, your hero must not change. He must have an appearance and trait which stay with him from book to book. Take for example The Hardy Boys or Harry Potter. These are series heroes that do not change.

If your series hero is a fat and blonde young woman who is a psychic and walks with a limp, for example, this description must stay with her from book to book in the series.

The Villain

The second character we will be looking at is the villain.
The villain is the no-good character that is important to the plot. He is either the chief adversary of the hero or the culprit. This is the character that is the cause of the conflict in the story. This is the character whose downfall the reader will hope for.

Appearance

You do not have to give the villain an ugly appearance. In fact, the villain may be better-looking than the hero. You will create the villain through his action—not his physical appearance. The physical appearance of the villain is important. The reader needs to know how he looks. But no matter what physical appearance you give to a character, if that character is not doing anything bad (cause the conflict), he is not the villain. Action is identity. The reader will identify the villain from the hero by their actions.

Name of the villain

You must choose a name that fits the villain well.   Before you give the villain his name,   take into consideration the personality you will give him. The villain's name and personality should not sound out of kilter to the reader.   For example: Which of the following names would you give a belligerent and heartless villain who is a drug dealer: Junior or Scarface? The name 'Scarface' would do better.

Let us say that your villain is a handsome and rich business man but who is a cunning, greedy swindler. Which of the following names would fit him better: Richard or Dogman?   The name Richard would do better. The name 'Dogman' sounds like a term for a street criminal.

Motive of the villain

The actions of the villain must be gratuitous or unfair. Whatever is his motive for action, it must not be justifiable.   If you justify the villain's motive (particularly for the action which causes the conflict), your story no longer has a villain.

The villain may have an internal motive (example: greed, addiction, or a twisted desire to rape and mutilate young women) or an external motive (example: attempting to kill a witness).

You may let the reader know the motive of the villain before he acts or after he has acted.

Before: Let us say that you start your story showing Mike and his wife arguing. She threatens to divorce him. Mike thinks about what the divorce would cost him.   Right there and then he strangles his wife and dumps her body. In this approach, you show the villain's motive before he acts.

After: In this approach, you show the committing of the crime but delay revealing the motive of the villain until the conclusion of the story. This approach is typical in the writing of a mystery.

Series villain

If you are writing a series and will use the same villain from book to book, the trait of the villain should not change. For example: If he is ruthless, greedy and deceitful, he must stay that way until his defeat.

The villain as central character

The fact that you will have a villain does not mean that you will need to have a hero. You may write a story in which the central character is the villain. In such a story, the reader will hope for the downfall of the villain while sympathizing with his victim. Since there is no hero for the reader to rally behind to bring down the villain, the following are two ways you may show the end of the villain:

He self-destructs: In this approach, you show the villain's own plan backfire and destroy him.

His victim finds courage: In this approach you show the victim or one of the victims find the courage and smartness to stop the villain.

Psychological villain

Establishing a psychological villain for your story might be a little challenging, and your story will lack sense of reality if you do not appropriately demonstrate the psychological problem to the reader. To establish a psychological villain, you first need to understand enough about the psychological problem that you choose for your story. This means that you must do a research on the symptoms (behaviours that characterize the problem) and the possible solutions.

A psychological villain is a mental disorder that causes the problem (conflict) in a story. It creates an internal conflict. But it does not have to be the hero who has the psychological problem. Example: the hero is the son of the woman suffering from heroin addiction. Examples of a psychological villain are: depression, schizophrenia, and Alzheimer's.

End of the villain

Your story does not have to end with the death of the villain. The idea that the villain has to die is misleading. You may end your story with the villain changed into a good character, locked away for life, or—which may upset the reader—simply escapes.

Villain as hero

If your story is dealing with an internal conflict, the villain may be the hero himself. For example, your story is about a man fighting his heroin addiction. The reader will root for him to defeat his addiction. Obviously, the villain is self. So the hero and the villain is the same.

Background Characters

The third character we will be looking at is the background character.

Background characters are characters used in a scene but have no role in the plot of the story. They are exactly where they are—in the background.

Look at the following example:

Detective Collin shadows Harry through the rosy crowd on the white-sand beach.

How many characters are in this scene? There is Harry, Detective Collin, and the crowd. Which is in the background? The answer is 'the crowd.' The crowd is in the scene but has no role in what the story is about.

Background characters are not given a dialogue but they may be given sounds (example: John squeezes through the <u>crumbling passengers</u> standing in the train). They may also be given action (example: Little Mary Lou studies for the upcoming exam while <u>other children play</u> in the school yard).

The purpose of background characters is to embellish or enliven a scene. Let us say that your hero walks into a bar looking for the villain. To enliven the bar-scene you may want to put background characters in the bar, maybe four hairy-faced men at the bar counter in front the bartender and two other men smoking by the window.

Background characters must fit a scene well. What kind of background characters would you create in a scene at a train station? What kind of background characters would you create in a scene at a football game? You should ensure that the people you put in the background (how they look and what they are doing) fit into the scene.

Regarding background, you should add to it more than just humans. To the background in a scene, you may add <u>sound</u> (example: a TV playing while the killer enters the apartment to strangle the young damsel lying on the couch); you may add <u>smell</u> (example: reeking garbage on a dark street corner where Mike exchanges the illegal guns for cocaine); you may add <u>feeling</u> (example: cold wind blowing from the sea while David hugs Cindy on the shore); you may add animal (example: a barking dog across the dark street while Pat and Duke makes love in the parked car). You may add objects (example: books on a desk, two parked trucks in the dark alley).

The background points to the entire space surrounding the character or characters used to carry out a scene. Within such entire space you may put people, animals, insects, and/or objects.

The background is important when imparting a story. It helps to tell the story. So you should never leave it blank. You might ask: How does the background help to tell a story? To get the answer to this question visually, simply pick up a DVD movie in your home and start to watch it. Pay attention to the backgrounds in the scenes of the movie. You will notice that the activities in the background of each scene (example: snow falling or persons jogging by) are all arranged to tell the scene.

So you should embellish the background in every scene of your story. If you write that Fabian meets Tony on a street in the city, let the reader see the city too. Is the street busy with vehicles and pedestrians? Is it morning, midday, or night? Is it sunny, warm, or cold? Is the sky cloudless or cloudy? Are there small buildings or skyscrapers around?

When you let the reader see, feel, smell, and hear the surroundings of the character or characters in a scene, the scene will be more interesting to the reader.

One-Scene Characters

The fourth character we will be looking at is a one-scene character. A one-scene character is a character that appears only in one scene. Such character may or may not play a role in the plot. For example: The hero goes to a town in search of Screwface (the villain). The hero meets Screwface's ex-girlfriend and asks her where to find Screwface. She gives the hero an answer and after this scene, the reader does not meet the ex-girlfriend again. The ex-girlfriend is a one-scene character.

You do not have to plan beforehand on which character to put into one scene. Do not make any plan for this. If at the end of your story, a character happens to be in only one scene, just leave it as such.

A one-scene character is a minor character. But there is one exception where a one-scene character becomes a feature character. This exception typically occurs in a mystery. In most, if not all, mysteries, the murder victim appears in only one scene—the scene in which he or she is murdered—but throughout the entire story, the murder victim is a feature.

Characters and description

You must give description to your characters according to their roles or the scene in which you put them. For example, you cannot give a secretary at a law firm a strapless blouse and mini skirt while she is at work at the law firm. Here are some important tips:

1. You must remember the description you give each character. If you describe a character as blonde with short hair, it would be wrong to later write that she combs her black, long hair. Keeping track of what you write is important.

2. Do not repeat all the description of a character. You do not have to keep reminding the reader that, for example, Jane Smith's eyes are blue and she is portly. Some things about a character are not worth repeating often. The description that worth often repeat throughout a story are a character's name, particular way of speaking, and his habit.

3. Background characters must not be named. The only logical exception is when you put a famous person in the background. For example: Your hero walks into a crowded club where Justin Bieber is performing on stage.

4. You do not have to give a one-scene character a name. This might be too much of a description for a character that the reader will only meet once.

5. When you do not identify a character with a proper noun, you must keep identifying such character with a common noun that is a special description—for example: **the Old Man**. The reader will henceforth know that unnamed character as 'the Old Man.'

6. Except in a brief story (example: two pages long), your characters should not be narrowed to the conflict. You should break from the conflict with minor interests and show your characters doing other things— eat, sleep, fall in love, play, have sex, etc.—which will give variety to your story and interest the reader.

7. Do not kill your story by solving the conflict with a new character or an act of God. The conflict must be solved by a character that the reader has already known. If your story has a hero, he must solve the conflict, or the conflict must be solved mainly due to his action.

Writing Character Speeches

Many stories are written without speeches given to the characters. So what is the purpose of giving speech to a character in a story? The answer is clear: Speeches help to tell a story. Using speech, you can show a character verbally expressing his thoughts or conversing with another character.

You may use indirect speeches or direct speeches. Both do not have the same effect on the reader. Direct speeches in a story let the reader listen to the characters instead of constantly to the narrator. In other words, a direct speech gives personal voice to a character. For example, it would be more interesting to let the reader listen to Andy asking Julia to marry him instead of writing that Andy asks Julia to marry him. Direct speeches even allow you to demonstrate the emotions of the characters better. Look at the following comparison:

Indirect speech in the scene: *Andy kneels in front Julia on the pavement and passionately he looks up in her blue eyes. He asks her to marry him. Julia, overwhelmed with joyful emotion, says yes.*

Direct speech in the scene: *Andy kneels in front Julia on the pavement and passionately he looks up in her blue eyes. "Will you be my wife, Julia?" he asks.*

"Yes," Julia overwhelmed with joyful emotion, replies.

As you can see, a character that speaks connects to the reader more than a mute character. But to speak or not to speak is the decision of the author. The genre or length of the story does not decide this. Only the author decides whether it is best to use indirect speech, direct speech, or the combination of both when writing a story.

Direct speeches come in five types—dialogues, monologues, soliloquys, apostrophes, and asides. Closet drama (stories for reading) use mostly dialogues and soliloquys. The other three types of speeches are suited for drama (plays, films, and radio/TV shows). Each type of speech uses the character in a different way, as examined in the following:

Dialogues

A dialogue is a conversation between at least two characters. If you write a scene with two characters and only one speaks, the scene does not have a dialogue. The characters must speak to each other—no matter the length or whether it is face to face or by telephone—in order to have a dialogue. Dialogues are most used in stories when compared to the other types of speeches.

The purpose of a dialogue is to help tell the story. So a dialogue must contribute something to the story. Apart from helping the plot or a minor course of events in the story, a dialogue may serve to simply give the reader a joke. You may use a dialogue to give the reader a backstory (example, the old king tells his son about the battle that caused the current enmity between his kingdom and the other). You may use dialogues to show how the characters feel about each other; how they individually think about the problem they face, etc. A dialogue is not just to say to the reader 'here is a conversation between two characters.' Whatever the characters say to each other must give the reader something new—no matter how minor the detail—to think about as she reads. Also, you should not just put any words in the mouths of characters and say to the reader 'that is dialogue.' Does everyone in the world speak with the same vocabulary? Absolutely not. The words a character uses must fit him well. Let us examine rules of dialogue through two examples below:

A street gangster: Your character is a street gangster. The way he speaks must represent the way one would expect a person in a street gang to speak. So you have a scene in which your street gangster walks toward a bench where a man is sitting. Will he ask the man: "Can you please shift over on the bench so I can sit, sir?" Or will he say to the man: "Hey, dude, shift over." The latter fits him better.

<u>A poor and uneducated man:</u> Your character is a poor and uneducated man. The words you put in his mouth must represent a poor and uneducated person. His use of words must lack proper grammar. For example: He says "I have not hurt nobody," instead of the grammatically correct way: "I have not hurt anybody." To tell the reader that the man is uneducated and not demonstrating it is a failure.

Setting affects dialogues

The major setting of your story might need to play an important part in dialogues. If you set your story on a real place, the dialogues should fit the place. For example: Your story is set in Jamaica. How do Jamaicans speak? Will you have a Rastafarian greets: "Welcome to Jamaica, sir" or will he greets "Welcome to Jamaica, man." The latter fits him better.

If you set your story on a law firm, how do attorneys speak when discussing cases? The story would be set on a 'specialized background.' Remember that attorneys (or lawyers) use technical terms—jargons of the legal profession—when dealing with business. How many of the technical terms in the legal profession do you know to write your story from the angle of an attorney?

Obviously, you must take into your consideration each character and the major setting (minor settings too, if your story shifts between different countries) before writing dialogues. If a dialogue does not match the setting or a character, your story—or the scene that the dialogue is in—will be out of kilter.

Handling a long dialogue

In a scene with a long dialogue between two characters, you do not have to keep identifying each character after a speech. For example, if the dialogue is between David and Sandy, you do not have to— after you have established the setting and mood—keep writing that 'David says' after his speech. You can pause telling the reader when David speaks and when Sandy speaks, because the reader would have already known. Look at the following illustration:

"It's a lovely morning," Sandy remarks as she sits beside David on the iron bench besides the still river.

"Indeed," David agrees, glancing Sandy with a smile before looking back at the peaceful body of water in front them.

Sandy crosses her slender legs in the long, blue jeans she wears and combs her short and blonde hair back with her left fingers. She takes in a deep breath and looks out at the river where two ducks sit quietly on top the water. Several seconds pass by before her thin lips move apart again.

"You seem to love out here," she says with a concise look at the rising sun before looking back at David.

"I do," David utters and closes back his lips with a smile while still pointing his blue eyes at the river. "I spend my mornings out here each week before I go to work."

"Me too," Sandy reveals. "The serenity of this garden: It's the most relaxing place in London. I haven't been here for a long while. I assume you are new to this place."

"Yep," David tells her with a glance in her green eyes. "I moved into the white mansion on Sixth Avenue just two weeks ago."

"In the mansion?" Sandy utters with raised eyebrows to show a pleasant surprise.

"Do you live nearby?" David asks and crosses his long legs in his blue jeans while pushing his hands into the pockets of his black sweater and now looking back at Sandy.

"Yes," Sandy replies, turning directly to this new and handsome young man in the area.

She finds his company most pleasant already. His short brown hair, cut to cover his forehead, and his neat appearance, along with his pert and slightly thick lips, drags her interest in him. His display of humility is hugging her emotion with what feels to her like invisible hands. *Is this love at first sight—so fast?* She wonders.

"I love golf," Sandy utters, almost frightened by her own words which seem to have passed from her mouth by themselves.

"Golf?" David asks with a slight smile.

"Yes, I am a golf player. Do you like golf?"

"Yes, I am a lover of the sport. Why do you ask?"

"Silly me. Why should a female like me want to play a man's game?"

"It's not just a man's sport. It's a fun sport for men and women."

"How many times per week do you have this fun?" Sandy asks.

"Hmm? Are you inviting me out to a session of golf?"

"Maybe. Anyway, my name is Sandy."

"Ok. I'm David."

David glances at his wrist watch. He takes in a deep breath and stands up six feet tall.

"I really have to go," he tells Sandy.

"Sure," Sandy says with a beam as David heads off.

Sandy takes in a deep breath. She watches David walks toward a black Honda motorbike about sixty feet away, admiring the motion of his rotund buttocks in his jeans. *He is one loaf of bread,* she thinks to herself.

"Yes!" she shouts with a wide smile that exposes her white teeth. "I want to play golf with you!"

But her words are blocked from David's sense of hearing by the earphones he has pushed in his ears. But Sandy knows she will meet this adorable guy again, tomorrow morning by the river.

As you can see in part of the dialogue, the need to tell the reader when David is speaking and when Sandy is speaking is not a must. Once the reader can clearly identify which character is speaking, there is no need to keep saying 'he says' or 'she says.' However, this is something that you must do briefly in a dialogue. If you take too long to get back to showing the reader which character is speaking, the reader might start losing track.

Monologues

A monologue is a lone speech by a character. It is not a speech made in response to another character or to be responded to by another character. It is a lone speech, though the character does not necessarily have to be alone. In a play, the actor speaks directly to the audience but does not converse with anyone who might say something from the audience. In a film or television show, the actor may be instructed to look in the camera now and again while mologuizing. This helps the viewer to get the feeling of being directly spoken to.

A monologue is both a literary device and a dramatic device. It is a tool designed to achieve a particular effect on the reader or audience. When you give a monologue to a character, you put the character and the reader face to face, figuratively, and give the reader the satisfying feeling of being spoken to by the character. The reader will feel 'recognized.' A part from this, the purpose of a monologue is to help tell the story. If it is not going to provide the reader with any new piece of information in understanding the progress of the story, it will be pointless.

When should a monologue be used? You may include a monologue anywhere in a story you are writing—in the opening scene, any middle scene, or even in the closing scene. But before you write a monologue, ensure that you first answer this question: What do you want the character to say to nobody else but the reader? Using a monologue, you may have the character express to the reader an opinion, intention, hidden detail or emotion.

A monologue is only suitable for a story written from the third person point of view. Why so? The third person point of view allows the writer to tell the thoughts of any character in the story; thus it is easy to include a monologue. On the other hand, the first person point of view only allows the writer to tell the thoughts of the 'I' character. Therefore giving a monologue to another character (where such character speaks to the reader) is impossible. Apart from the 'I' character, the writer cannot show a character speaking directly to the reader. As a matter of fact, even the 'I' character should not be given a monologue.   The monologue would not make sense due to the fact that the first person point of view is already, technically, a monologuizing act of the 'I' character.

You may write a monologue using the first person point of view, second person point of view, or third person point of view. Look at the following scene with a monologue using all viewpoints:

Jordon strolls into the office. He closes the door behind him. Now alone, he stands at the window. "You may think I don't love her. I do. Soon she will come to me and stay in my arms, where she belongs."

With the author clearly showing that the character is alone, the reader easily sees that the character is speaking to her. A monologue is at times confused with a soliloquy. The difference is that a monologue is a lone speech by a character to an audience or to another character. A soliloquy, on the other hand, is:

Soliloquy

A soliloquy is a speech in which a character is alone and speaks his or her thoughts aloud. The character is not speaking to anyone. A soliloquy may be written using the first person, second person, or third person point of view. It may be written incorporating two or all the three point of views. Look at the following scene with a soliloquy which uses only the first person point of view:

Otasha arrives at home early from school. She opens the front door of her parents' house and enters the living room. The big house is silent and there is an absence of her mother's humming from the kitchen which was usual at this time of the evening. Otasha strolls into the kitchen to no sight of her mother.

"I wonder where Mother is," she says. "She is not here in the kitchen and dinner is not yet ready. Maybe she is in the bathroom. Well, I guess I will have to just sit here and wait till she comes back."

Now look at the following scene with a soliloquy which uses all three point of views:

Antonius stands alone on the top of a hill two miles from the mount on which Princess Fiona is immured by Evil Count. A deep river, booby straps, and spiky stones lie between him and Evil Count's dwelling.

"She must be scared, worried and tormented inside that hell of a place," he thinks out with a low voice and gazing eyes. "She has to be. O, Fiona, how I am concerned for you. But I won't stand back and do nothing. I have to save you, no matter what."

Apostrophe

An apostrophe is an address to an absent or imaginary person. It may also be an address to God or to something without life. Particularly short, an apostrophe is often a digression in a speech. Otherwise it stands alone. On the question of how to write an apostrophe, the following examples demonstrate ways:

<u>As a digression in a speech:</u>   *"She must be scared, worried and tormented inside that hell of a place," he thinks out with a low voice and gazing eyes. "She has to be. O, Fiona, how I am concerned for you. But I won't stand back and do nothing. I have to save you, no matter what."*

The use of apostrophe can be easily identified in this speech above because the character digresses to address an absent person with the following lines:

"O, Fiona, how I am concerned for you." The other line is: *"I have to save you, no matter what."* Fiona is absent.

<u>As an address to an imaginary person:</u> *"You are somewhere out there, the woman to take the crown of princess and reign by my side. Somehow, I feel you. You are in this kingdom, and I will ferret until I lay sight on you and know you."*

The character is obviously addressing an imaginary person in the speech. The person, a princess, only exists in the scene in the character's imagination. So the speech is an apostrophe.

<u>As an address to God:</u> "O God, save us!"

What the character says may or may not constitute a prayer. The above (on previous page) constitutes a prayer but would not if the character had only exclaimed 'O God!"

As an address to an inanimate thing: *"O hate, why are thou love's adversary?"*

Aside

Aside is a dramatic device in which a character says something that is regarded as unheard by another character or characters in a play. Aside represents unspoken thoughts or is an address to the audience. An aside is used in a play that is particularly a comedy. This is because of its function. The following paragraph gives an example of an aside in a play:

Rufus and Matilda are seated at a table on stage. The audience is watching. In this scene of the play, Rufus and Matilda are on a date in a restaurant. Both are smiling and looking at each other at the table. Rufus says "you are an ugly hog" with the smile still on his face. (The audience is amused as Matilda is still sitting at the table and smiling, not supposed to hear what Rufus said. The audience must see Rufus' words as representing unspoken thoughts).

The words of an aside may be written from the first person, second person, or third person point of view. Above, Rufus spoke from the second person point of view. If he was to speak from the third person point of view, he would most likely look to the audience and address the audience by saying "she is an ugly hog."

The use of aside in closet drama would most likely be confusing on the side of the reader. To have an aside, your story would have to show a character that speaks, is heard by another character, but is not heard by such character. Obviously, the reader would get confused! So it is not a good idea to attempt an aside in a story for reading. As a matter of fact, an aside is defined specifically as a dramatic device, not a literary device. In addition to this, dictionaries define aside as something said on a stage.

Scenes

Here are some important questions and answers about scenes.

What is a scene?

A scene is the time and place of a particular incidence in a story.

What must go into my first scene?

This will depend on what you want to start the story with. Will you start the story with the setting (exposition), character development, or conflict?

Conflict:

If you decide to start the story with the conflict, then the conflict will begin the first scene. Example: You start with the killer—villain—entering the victim's house to commit the crime that will start the conflict of the story.

Character development:

If you start with character development, then this will begin your first scene. Example: You start by describing the trait of the hero—such as the following example:

His name is Jake, fearless cop in the notorious city of Downtown Kingston, Jamaica. He never walks alone. He is always accompanied by his loaded friend—a clean and spanked Smith and Wesson pistol. He knows no boundaries set by those who are not doing good. He flinches not to scowled faces of hardened criminals. Where the bad guys are he will go. Wherever they run, he will track them down. He never makes an empty threat to bad guys. He keeps order. He keeps the law. You mess with him, you will mess yourself. His name is known all around the city. He is--JACK THE COP.

How long should a scene be?

You should not decide how long or short a scene will be before you start. It is not a good idea to say that, for example, "this scene will be one page long." In fact, you must not focus on the length of a scene before you write. There is no rule on how long or short a scene must be. Once you have fulfilled the purpose of the scene, the scene ends.

What must be the purpose of a scene?

The purpose of a scene is either to help carry out the plot or help carry out a minor interest.

Minor interest: Not every scene has to relate to the plot. So its purpose would be to carry out a minor interest—something of interest other than the focus of the story. For example: A love-making scene in a story that is about a black family struggling to live peacefully in a racist, white community. The love-making scene (probably between the black man and his wife) does not contribute to the plot, but it enlivens the story as a minor interest.

Help the plot. A scene that helps the plot is a scene which pushes the plot somewhat toward its climax.

How do I start and end a scene?

What you must do when you start a scene is to fulfill the purpose of the scene. For example: Why are you writing that Paul meets Cindy at a dark corner at 11:30 pm in the night? Once you have fulfilled the purpose of the scene, move on to a new scene or chapter. You must continue this way until you reach the final scene, called the 'closing scene.'

What are the basics of scene writing?

When establishing a scene, it is best to tell who, why, where, when, and how. All these five elements are to exist for a complete portrayal of a scene. Let us look at each element carefully:

Who: Typically, a scene has one or more characters. So you must clearly show the reader the person or persons who are in the scene—whether you are identifying   them with common nouns or proper nouns. But it is possible to write a scene without any character, such as a scene of an evacuated city being battered by a storm.

<u>Why</u>: You must show the purpose of the scene to the reader. If you write a scene with Elizabeth chasing Bobby with a broom stick, the question of why must be shown to the reader. The purpose of the scene may be shown through dialogue or direct narration (you tell the reader).

The question of why also applies to the scene-after-scene construction of the story itself. For example: Why do you have a love-making scene at this point in the story? Every scene is a building block in the telling of the story. Scene after scene are linked together to tell the entire story. If scene 1 shows Donovan jumping through the window of his house when a drug dealer broke in and killed his wife and daughter, why would you have scene 2 showing Donovan making love to a beautiful woman? Scene 2 does not seem to fit in with the constructing of the story. The question of why you are putting Donovan in a love-making scene after his tragic lost in scene 1 would have to be logically explained to the reader.

So before you write a scene, you need to answer the question of why you are going to write it. In other words, what is the purpose of the scene? Remember that a scene does not stand alone. Whatever is its purpose, it must add something to the progress of the story.

<u>Where:</u> A scene without a location is just 'somewhere or 'anywhere' in the telling of the story. This is not satisfying to the reader. You must give a place to each scene in your story. The reader is at a lost if you only describe two characters talking. Where are they while talking? Specifically, are they in a car, office, bus park, etc?

<u>When:</u> Showing when is giving the scene a time. If you describe Alice lying in the arm of Marcus on the lawn in their front yard, you need to give a time to the scene. So you may describe the sun descending over the mountain. The <u>descending sun</u> puts a time into the scene which says to the reader 'it is evening.'

<u>How:</u> Showing 'how' is to show the connection of the scene to the entire story. How does this scene shape the story base on where you put it? Every scene must be connected to the telling of the story. Is the scene contributing   to the plot (main sequence of the story) or a

minor interest? What does the scene reveal to the reader?

There are two scenes in a story that show how, whether or not a writer gives them special attention prior to writing. They are the <u>beginning scene</u> and the <u>closing scene</u>. One shows how the story starts and the other shows how the story ends.

How do I actually compose a scene?

Before you write a scene,   you must first clearly understand where you are and where you are going next with the story. By understanding what you want to happen next, you will easily compose the next scene.

Make sure, of course, that you have a mood for the scene you are going to write.   The mood (the feeling the reader will get while reading) is established by your choice of words when narrating the scene. So your 'writing tone' is crucial to establishing the mood. You will set the mood of a scene either through the setting (how you describe the time and place) or the characters (how you describe their thoughts, dialogue, and actions).

What should I do if I feel I cannot complete a scene?

This happens to every writer. You are writing and suddenly you lose idea of what else to write. What you can do is to take in a deep breath and pause, or take a walk, before you resume. If this does not work, maybe you need to take an entire day (or more)   break from your writing. This is because you were probably writing so long; you are now experiencing a 'burn out.' A long break should refresh your mind.

If after a long break you still cannot continue, what you are hereby recommended to do is to examine the scene you were writing for error. Maybe you have written the scene into a dead-end, and now you have no logical means to get out. But do not just sit there and say to yourself that you don't know what to do. What you will have to do is to simply re-write the scene in a new way.

What must go into the final scene?

The final scene carries whatever you have decided to close the story on. For example: If you have decided to close the story showing the hero vanquishing the villain in a final battle, this will make the final scene.   If you want to close the story showing the main characters getting back to their normal lives after a turbulent period, this will go into the final scene.

The final scene must bring a sense of satisfaction to the reader—the satisfaction both for reading your book and for how the story ends.

Chapters

Questions and Answers

What is a chapter?

A chapter is one section of a text which deals with a portion of what the text is about. Typically, each chapter carries a major development in the progress of the text.

A chapter is typically identified by a heading bearing a number–example: Chapter One or Part One. The number in the heading shows the reader which chapter she is at.

What must go into the first chapter of a story?

The first chapter is the initial block in the building of your story. You must use the first chapter to:

(a) Develop the setting (time and place of the story)
(b) Introduce some of the characters
(c) Start the conflict (if the story will carry one)
(e) Set the general mood of the story (example: comical)

All these four elements should commence in the first chapter, which set the story in motion and allow the reader to have an early and proper understanding of the story. If your first chapter is short, you should bring out said four elements in at least the first two chapters.

How many pages should a chapter have?

There is no standard amount of pages a chapter should have. One chapter of a story may have two pages, another chapter has twenty pages, a next chapter has fourteen pages, etc. The important thing is that you will create each chapter by completing a section of the plot–even if that section happens to be only one page.

How do I end a chapter?

Except for the final chapter, you may end each chapter with a cliffhanger. A cliffhanger is a situation which is exciting because the reader does not know what is going to happen next. Example: *Paul strolls toward the door in response to the gentle knock. He turns the knob and pulls the slab door open and finds himself staring in the barrel of a loaded pistol.* By ending the chapter here, you make the reader curious to read the next chapter.

Should I decide beforehand on how many chapters my story should have?

Not necessarily, because this might limit you or cause you to stretch the story unnecessarily to satisfy the amount of chapters you have pre-set.

Why put chapters in a book?

Chapters are put in a text to make it easier to be understood by the reader. An example of this is the Bible. Maybe you can remember been to a church and heard the religious minister said something like "Jesus says in Matthew chapter 4 verse 10...." Now imagine that the book of Matthew did not have chapters. How would that minister easily lead his congregation to the quote from Jesus? Obviously, chapters make a text easier to be handled by the reader.

What must go into my final chapter?

You will use the final chapter to bring the conflict of the story to an end. The end of the conflict is the end of the story. If the story does not have a conflict, you will use the final chapter to bring to conclusion the open subject (typically, a lesson) of the story. The final chapter is expected to carry the conclusion of the story.

How To Write A Novel

A novel is an extended literary work of fiction—typically resulting in a book with a long reading time. When you will write a novel, do not think that you will write a long book. If you think this way, you will be focusing on how many pages you can write—which is not where your focus should be. Instead, your focus should be on the story itself. You will focus on building a story, not building pages.

To achieve writing a novel, the first intention is to delay the conclusion of the plot. The longer you take to conclude the story, the longer the story becomes. You will give to your story more than what you would with a short story. What more exactly? You will give more details through use of the following:

Part of speeches: adjectives and adverbs.

Poetic devices: simile, metaphor, personification, onomatopoeia, hyperbole, etc.

Minor interests: sex, eating, romantic attraction etc.

Minor conflicts: Courses of events (difficulties, disagreements, etc.) outside the major conflict.

Description: A carefully placed exposition may be useful. The following are the things you will have to describe more:

Emotion: Your characters will experience different emotions through the story. Spend more time on a character's emotions through elongation. You may even give an entire scene to the thoughts (or soliloquy) of a character. In a short story you may write:

Paul thinks about his family before he leaps from the bridge to his own death.

But in a novel you will need to spend more time on what Paul is thinking, so that you will give more to the story. You may write that Paul thinks about his son and the possible emotional pain his suicide will bring to the boy; then Paul thinks on his wife and some memories he shared with her; and then Paul thinks on the reason for his decision. Between these thoughts, you may elongate the scene by describing the setting of the scene---the river below the bridge, the air, sound, etc.

Because you want a long story, you will avoid just using one word— example, sad—to describe an emotion. Instead you will show the character's emotion to the reader in details. You may use a paragraph (or more) to describe the sadness of the character instead of the one word 'sad.'

Dialogues: You will make dialogues longer than you would with a short story. (However, not every dialogue has to be long). Also spend more time describing to the reader what each character is doing in a dialogue. Within a dialogue, you will have your characters do and say extra things—example: pause and think, comb hair, chat a little about each other's clothes, etc—and you should describe their changing facial expressions and body language.

Actions: You will stretch your story by describing actions of your characters in details. Instead of omitting some actions of your characters, you will write what each character is doing—step by step. For example, instead of writing that:

(a) *David wakes up and heads to the shower. After a warm bath he gets dressed and strolls from his apartment into the morning rush hour.*

You may make this scene longer with more details as follows:

(c) *David's eyelids slowly pull apart, ending a long slumber, and glance at the analogue clock on the wall in his bedroom. He sits up on the side of the bed and drops his feet on the blue rug on the tiled floor. Combing his fingers through his tousled brown hair, he takes in a deep breath. Few seconds pass before he stands up and adjusts his black boxers, the only piece of clothes he slept in through the night.*

David groggily steps toward the window and shifts the white curtain for a look through the slightly misty panes at the rising sun. After a glance at his dew-damped motorbike in the drive way, he strolls to the bathroom. His shower lasted only several minutes and feeling refreshed, he heads back to the bedroom. Combing his hair in front the mirror, David glances down at the picture of his wife whom he will pick up at the airport. Her business trip has kept her away for the past three weeks. Today she is coming home.

Clothed in blue jeans, white T shirt, leather slippers and hair neatly combed back, David heads from the apartment into the morning rush hour.

As you can see in option (b), more details are added between David waking up and leaving his apartment, which lengthen the scene and thus the story.

However, you do not have to detail 'every' action of your characters. You can be selective in this regard.

Solution to the plot: Because you are writing a novel, you must delay the conclusion of the plot with the use of small difficulties (unfortunate coincidences) and twists. For example: Your story is about the Stewarts retaking control of a city. In the short story, you may bring the story to an end after showing David Stewart retaking the city. But for a novel, you may stretch the story to include internal rivalries among the Stewarts, war preparations, love affairs, betrayal, and them losing the city and retaking it again. You may also go into the history of the city through dialogues and/or exposition. This is careful elongation to achieve a novel.

Minor interests: You must create more minor interests than you would with a short story. Minor interests are small conflicts and enlivening activities (sex, dining, jealousy, etc.) outside the major conflict. Each minor interest, however, must fit into the story well.

Characters: A novel typically carries more characters, feature ones and minor ones. The development of each character in details (but not in one paragraph or scene) is useful for lengthening your story.

Settings: Remember, a story has two types of settings—the major one and the minor ones. But a novel may have more than one major setting.   Example: Your novel is about a boy who travels into the future to save his adult self from a fatal car crash. You write the story with a fully developed setting of the boy's present life and a fully developed setting of his future life, thus giving the story two major settings.

The term 'fully developed setting,' as used above, means a time and place furnished with a plot and characters.

Because you want a long story, you must go in-depth in your description of each minor setting. For example: Instead of writing that Randy enters the crowded train station and gets on a train to New York, you should give more information about the train station. What does it sound like to Randy as he enters it to buy a ticket? What is the feeling inside the place? Is there a queue?

Remember: A novel uses a complex plot and may be written with more than one major setting, plot, or even hero. An example of this is a novel that contains a backstory that is a full story from the main story.

Writing Literature for Radio or TV Drama

Writing for a radio or television drama can be as interesting as authoring a book. But the challenges are not all the same. The disparity is that 'closet drama' (literature for reading) is prepared differently from literature for a stage, radio or television drama. So what is the difference?

Closet Drama: With closet drama, the writer starts from a story idea to a manuscript, then to a book. The writer creates characters and shows them performing the speeches and actions along the storyline, thus having a self-contained story at the end of writing.

Drama: A drama is a dramatic work intended for performance by actors. So, unlike closet drama, the performance element—speeches and actions— of the written work are not executed within the work but externally by actors. A playwright starts from a story idea to a script, then to the performer (s). Regarding a radio or television drama, there is usually a writing staff. The writers start from a story idea—formed out of different ideas from members of the writing staff—to a script. The performance of the script is later done by actors under the instructions of a director. One or more members of the writing staff may supervise initial performance by the actors to get a feel of the effectiveness of the script and to offer suggestions, if needed, to the director.

It is important to state that literature for a radio drama is written somewhat different from literature for television drama. This is because television is an audiovisual medium while radio is audio. Speeches written for radio drama have to be more descriptive because the audience is not seeing the actors. For television, the speeches may be less descriptive, because the audience is visually getting aspects of the story—emotions, action, and settings.

A drama may be serialized or not. Those serialized are called drama series or serial drama. Many are set on a specialized background—such as crime investigation, court cases, or police detective work. To write for a drama using a specialized background will require you to first be knowledgeable of some applicable jargons or technical terms. So regarding a drama dealing with court cases, for example, what are some legal terms used by attorneys? When and how are such terms used? In order to write courtroom dialogues, you should have knowledge on jargons of the legal profession.

Writing for a radio drama:

Let us first look at writing for a radio drama. The big rule about radio broadcast is that everything has to be delivered in audio alone. So a script for a radio drama has to be speech-focused in how it is written. The script must be written to be performed using one of the two following methods:

Narrator and actors: With this approach, the listeners will hear a person describing the story (either from the first person or third person point of view) and actors doing the dialogues, soliloquys, and monologues.

As the writer (but there is usually a team of writers for a drama) it is your duty to write the speeches for the narrator and the speeches for the actors. Look at the following example:

Narrator: The needles of the old wall clock ticked miserably toward midnight. I have been waiting out of patience: four long hours and John has not yet arrived from the airport. My eyelids weighed down gradually and slumber, like a romantic lover, began taking my weary body into sweet unconsciousness. Then in the split of a second there was a knock at the front door.

[Sounds of door knocked, footsteps followed by opening of door]

Actress: "John, I have waited most desperately for you to come. I almost believe your flight was cancelled."

Actor: "No sweetheart. A few stops to clear snow in the road lengthened the time of my journey, but I made it here safely."

Actors only: With this approach, the listeners will understand the drama through speeches by the actors. The absence of a narrator means that the entire story is understood by what the actors say (dialogues, soliloquys, and monologues). This means that you will have to write more descriptively, putting information you would have written for a narrator into the very utterances of the actors. This takes caution as the information is not delivered in the same way. For example, you are going to write a scene with a stranger bouncing on Mike in his office and shooting him. A narrator would easily tell the listeners that a stranger enters Mike's office with a gun. But since there is no narrator, you will have to deliver the same information to the listeners through speeches of the actor (s). So you may write the scene as follows:

Mike: "Who are you? How did you get in my office? Please, don't shoot!" (Sound of fired pistol).
Mike's secretary: [her footsteps enter the office]: "I heard a shot, Sir. What happened?"
Mike: "Call the police, the ambulance too. I have been shot."
Secretary: "By who, Sir? I see no one."
Mike: "By a fat man wearing a black felt hat and brown coat. He escaped through the rear door. Don't just stand there, Maggie, get me help!"

As you can clearly see in the example above, the listeners—based on Mike's speeches—know that a stranger bounced on Mike in his office, that the stranger is wearing a felt hat and brown coat, and that he escapes through the rear door.

Apart from speeches, you will have to write emotions and actions. It will be up to the actors to bring such emotions (anger, dejection, etc.) to life when they speak. But it will not be up to the actors to bring the actions to life. The actors doing a radio drama may be sitting at microphones as they speak. So it is up to the producer to bring the actions (footsteps, door closing, etc.) to life using sound effects.

Along with emotions, each actor will have to bring to life the given personality of the character they play. This is part of their duties when performing the script. But the actors cannot do this alone. As writer, you will have to first write to fit the personality of each character. For example, a character in the drama series is tactless and mean. You will have to first write to fit a tactless and mean person in order for the actor to properly speak and sound tactless and mean. So, obviously, the personality of each character in the drama is maintained by both the writer and the actor.

Writing for a television drama:

As a writer, you probably wonder what it would feel like writing for your favourite television drama series. There are two popular types of television drama series that might come to mind:

Sitcom: A sitcom is a comedy based on situations that could arise in day-to-day life. Many sitcoms are set on the day-to-day lives of a household with each episode dealing with a new matter (s) among the household. Sometimes a matter encompasses two episodes and so the first episode will end with a 'to be continued' text that shows that the matter continues into the following episode.

The episodes for a sitcom are really short stories, because each has its own plot which begins and ends at the close of the episode. This means that the viewers do not have to wait episodes after episodes to see a matter resolved. Though there is a new story to tell with each episode, the show maintains the same cast, traits, settings and theme. You may call such continuous portion of the show the 'arc.' Writing for a sitcom, no matter the plot for an episode, you will have to write to fit the arc.

Soap Opera:

Made for radio or television, a soap opera is a serialized programme which contains multiple matters to follow. A soap opera may be set on the lives of a group of people in a town. Unlike a sitcom, a soap opera typically has multiple matters which together continue from episodes to episodes. Matters come and go as the series progress.

Writing for a soap opera is a complex job. This is because the team of writers must determine and maintain the courses of the multiple matters, some of which are usually connected as factors of the other. The writers must also manage character personalities and actions as they write. The story writing tips in this book are applicable to writing a soap opera.

How To Write Children Books

Children books are defined as books published for pre-adult readers. The term 'children' is not a genre but is an 'age category,' which carries rules you will not find in other age categories. The following are some useful tips on writing books for children.

Use simple language

A children book should be written using a <u>simple vocabulary</u>. This means that the words you use in description and dialogues must be of the simplest forms. Do not use a college or university-level language to write to children.

Metaphor

Do not use many metaphors in your writing. Remember that a metaphor cannot be taken literally. Since children, particularly those under age 10, normally take things they read literally, your book might have a confusing effect on them if it contained too many metaphors.

Simile

The use of similes is mind-improving for young readers. Similes draw children to compare things and thus excite them. Look at the following example of a simile:

While the other boys were fast on the play field, Little Pento was <u>as low as a turtle</u>.

The purpose of a simile, of course, is to make a description more interesting to the reader.   So use similes in your book; the children will love it.

Onomatopoeia

Onomatopoeia is the use of words that imitate the sounds they refer to. Examples: peep, whoosh.   Because children love reading the sounds of things, the application of onomatopoeia to your story is very important. The use of onomatopoeia in children stories is valuable because phonics (the sounding of letters) is an essential part of beginners' literacy education.

Writing For Children under Age 4

If you are targeting children under age 4, your book should be written with minimum or no sentence. This is because children this young are—for the most part—not readers but students to reading. They are the youngest of readers and are still learning the alphabet and how to construct simple sentences. So your book should not be written with full text. Instead the book would be better if written with single words that identify things, places, and people. For example: Let us say your book is about teaching children different kinds of fruits. Instead of writing "This is a mango" under the picture of a mango, you would simply write "mango." It is much easier for the child to look at the picture of the mango accompanied by its name and say 'mango,' than to struggle through an entire sentence to get the same message. So if you want them to know a thing, person, or place it is better to write only its name. A single word gets to the point when writing to children age 4 or younger.

Another important thing when you are writing for children this young is that your book should use bigger fonts. Size 12 is an average font for books. But for the youngest readers the recommended font size is 14. It is not that children have bad eyesight why this is recommended. Their eyesight is the sharpest. The purpose of using bigger fonts in children books has always being part of facilitating the comprehension of words.

Writing For Children over Age 4

Children over age 4, generally, are able to understand a message given through a sentence. This is because, unlike age 2, they are able to understand words grouped   together (called sentence) to give a message. So you may write your book with full text—sentences and paragraphs. So rather than writing 'mango' under the picture of a mango, you may write 'This is a mango.'

Colours and Illustration

Illustration is very useful where necessary. Not everything a child will understand properly from a text, and therefore some things have to be pictured to them. For example: Your book is about different types of rodents. Text alone for this book would do a poor job. It would not be clear enough to write "a beaver is a brown, furry animal with strong teeth and can move about both on land and in water." While this would get a child thinking, the book would educate the child better with the picture or drawing of a beaver. The point is that a text-only book is less interesting (even less educating) to a child when compared to a colourful book with illustration. You might remember how as a child you felt better when the subjects or characters of a book were pictured to you.

Colours are also important in reaching children with your book. A child will choose a book from many books on a shelf because of its colourful cover.

Choosing a topic

What do you want to tell children with your book? Before you can answer this question, you must be able to clearly identify children topics from adult topics. This is important. Whatever your book will be about, it must comply with the two following principles:

(a) Age appropriate (b) Educational.

Regarding age appropriateness, children books are expected to be of positive influence. While books for adults are written with violence, revenge, suicide, and sex, children books—on the other hand—are expected to shape each young reader's mind in a positive way. A children book must be positive. When a child reads your book, the child should be thinking positively as a result. The deepest extent a children book should go into the negative is to make a child feel sad, usually because a loveable character dies. But it would be inappropriate for your book to leave children thinking about suicide or revenge, for example, after reading. Your entire book might not be saying revenge, but a particular scene might be unintentionally encouraging it.

Children will grow up and some of them will—no matter how most of us wish not to imagine it—become murderers, thieves, rapists, and scum bags. But we would make tomorrow's adults worse than today's if we stopped keeping children books positive.

Regarding education, there are some topics that children are to be educated on and others to be left until they are in adolescence or adulthood. Topics such as dating, sexual techniques, marriage, and politics—just to name a few—are normally kept out of children literature.

Every children book, fiction or nonfiction, should be centered on education. The topic you choose does not have to be an academic one, but it should be making a contribution to child development. You must choose an educational topic and tell it in an entertaining way. Not the other way around where your book is entertaining but has no educational value.

Setting

Setting establishes time and place. When you are writing fiction for children, you need to put your story in a time and place that are familiar or fascinatingly new. You must give your story a setting that will excite the young reader and brightens his or her imagination.

Avoid giving a nebulous or dull setting. A dull setting is one that children generally do not find interesting in real life—such as a law firm, dental clinic, accounting firm, or hospital. Why would you want to set a children story in an accounting firm? Children in real life are not interested in what happens in an accounting firm. First understanding children's interests before you write for them makes you a better children book author.

Characters

Characters for children books must be handled differently from characters for books targeting adults. For a children book, the characters should not be acting or speaking profanely. This rule also applies to the way the characters are described and illustrated.

The personality you give each character—especially the central character—should be of the type that children generally love. Children generally love a very funny or adventurous character, no matter the plot. The more adventurous or funnier one or more characters are, the more enjoyable they will find the book.

Children generally love animal characters. So if you chose to tell your story using animal characters, this might be much better than using human characters. A story with talking animals, talking trees, talking fruits, interests a child more than a story with—which they experience every day—talking people. A story you will write can have a mixture of the characters, example: talking pigs and human characters. Personification in children stories is obviously effective.

Starting Your Story

When writing fiction for children, try to make your book grab the interest of the young readers very early. You need to try achieving this with the very first sentence of your book. Below are two famous starting phrases which have built the reputation of immediately catching children's attention, which you probably remember in books you have read as a child:

'Long ago in a far, far land…."

'Once upon a time…..."

You are not herein encouraged to use any of the above phrases to start your own story. Such starting phrases have become too common and overused. You should be creative and start your story in your own interesting way.

Starting your story with an exclamation is one effective tool to grab children interest immediately. Look at the following example:

"Look!" shouts Peggy.

Old Grandma Mattie turns from the washing pan and sees Peggy pointing at a green lizard in the big ackee tree.

Ending a children Story

Children expect a happy ending to any story.   Such expectation comes naturally from children, whether they are reading a story themselves or listening to an adult telling one. This is why many children stories end with the famous phrase 'and they live happily ever after.'

A happy ending makes a happy child.

So you should write your children story with a happy ending. In fact, a happy ending has become the rule with writing children stories.

The Story Ending

The ending of a story is the most important part to the reader. Therefore it must be handled with care. The end is the destination of the reader.

The end of the story must carry with it the end of the conflict. In fact, the end of the conflict is the end of the story. Once you bring the conflict to its end, the story basically ends. If you want to tell the reader what happens to the main characters after the conflict ends, do so in the same chapter that the conflict ends. Adding another chapter to the story after the conflict ends might be padding that will be of needless use to the reader.

If your story does not have a conflict, you should end the story once the lesson has been taught. A good example in support of this tip is the allegory *The Boy Who Cried Wolf*. The author ended the story once the boy (and the reader) has learnt the lesson that it is not fun to raise false alarm.

Upon the end of the story, there must not be an unanswered question in the mind of the reader. You must not leave the reader asking, for example: "But what happens to Little Peggy who is stranded in the woods?" To close your story properly, you must bring solution to the major conflict as well as to all small ones in your story.

HOW
TO
WRITE
NON-FICTION

Introduction

Nonfiction requires the use of truth and facts. It is the area of writing that requires the writer to inform or entertain on reality. Nonfiction requires the writer to stay within the realm of the real world. Any person, thing, or place that is dragged from the imagination will fail to fall under the definition of 'nonfiction.'

The writing of nonfiction is not any difficult than imaginary writing. On first thought, nonfiction would seem to put more weight on the writer. The writer has the task of ensuring that his work—for it to be nonfiction—accurately represents what had or is actually happening in real life. Fiction on the other hand, indulges the writer into a 'tell it as you please' offer. The writer therefore writes from his imagination, which is borderless. In this way fiction seems the easier path to the writer. But the truth is that both fiction and nonfiction are equally challenging. They both put rules on the writer who should follow them to make sense in his writing.

This section of the book is a guide for writing nonfiction. There are many types of nonfictional books, each carrying rules different from the others. To write each, you are to know the rules. But this book covers five important types and each has rules that the writer may follow to do best in his craft.

But what are the rules? And how many of the rules do you know?

One never stops learn. The rules you will read in this section of the book will either improve what you have already known about nonfiction or change the way you approach writing nonfiction.

With no need to lengthen this introduction, I urge you to continue.

Autobiography

Welcome to the section for how to write an autobiography.

Every day you provide others with information of yourself. Your choice of clothes, language, friends, career, religion, etc. each provides the public with a piece of information about you. But no action by you will put everything together like an autobiography. In this one account you can put all the pieces of information about your life in an orderly way for a full understanding of you.

An autobiography is an account of your own life, of the years you have already lived through, written by you. It is an account that everyone, if having the desire, should write.

An autobiography is not only for the rich or famous. The humblest of lives make some of the best autobiographies. The decision to write an autobiography should be yours entirely, written in your own vocabulary, from your own experiences and insight of yourself, and in your own space of time.

You should, however, follow some rules appertain to an autobiography. There are rules that apply 'before' you write and 'while' you write. We will begin with the rules that apply before you write. Here they are:

Have an overall idea for your account.

You must first identify an idea that your autobiography will be based on. This is important. It should not be difficult to do. To come up with an overall idea, you must ask yourself this question: Why do I want to tell others about my life? The answer you have will be the overall idea for the book.   For example, if you want to write the autobiography because you are now a successful business man who has had a poor childhood, then this will be the central idea of your account.

You should not just write a list of events of yourself from childhood to the present which only says to the reader 'here is a list of information about me' and leave the reader to find out the central understanding of the writing. Your account must have a purpose, which will form the central idea.

Some individuals have written their autobiography on the 'from rags to riches' idea. What's yours? The central idea for your autobiography does not have to have anything to do with money or riches. It is simply that central thing you want the reader to understand from your entire account.

Write only from personal experiences.

An autobiography is a firsthand account of your own life. So you will write your personal experiences—meaning events you have personally lived through from childhood to the present and people you have personally met. You will also, of course, write your beliefs and perceptions. You must show how or why those beliefs and perceptions have developed in you.

Write in the 'first person point of view.'

Because an autobiography is a firsthand account, it is best written from the first person point of view. Do not attempt writing your own life from the third person point of view.   Though this may be done, if you do, you will fail to bring the reader into a personal connection with you. Your account will sound as if it is someone else writing about you.

The first person point of view allows you to write as if you are speaking directly to the reader. The reader will feel as if she is listening to you directly.

What is the first person point of view?

When you write from the first person point of view, you become the "I" character in the entire account. Any writing in which one character is identified as 'I" is a writing written from the 'first person point of view.'

(For rules on the *first person point of view*, see page 23).

Write only from your own vocabulary

Write using words you would normally use if you were sitting in front someone and telling them about your own life. It is not a good idea to go and search for difficult words to use in order to appear more educated, for example, than you really are. An autobiography is a personal account. This means that the words you use must be from your own vocabulary. The words must represent the true you. Write a chapter and ask yourself: Do I really sound like that?

Write only one autobiography

Your autobiography should be unique, meaning that there is only one. It is ridiculous, subjectively stating, to write and publish an autobiography and later write and publish another one. There can be many biographies on you. But there should be only one autobiography. To ensure this, you should publish your autobiography in your older years. Age 45 is the best minimum age for publishing an autobiography. You may start write an autobiography from in your twenties. But it would be better to finalize and publish it at an older age when you have passed through many experiences or have passed through your heyday.

How To Begin

So you now understand the rules that apply before you write an autobiography. You are now ready to write. While writing the account of your life, you must apply the following rules:

The central idea of your account

Again, without being repetitive, you must first identify an idea that your autobiography will be based on. Some persons have written their autobiography on the idea of 'from rags to riches.' What's yours? Your idea does not have to be fancy. And it does not have to have anything to do with money or riches. But it must be the central thing you want the reader to get from your entire account. You should not just write a list of events about your life from childhood to the present to say to the reader 'that's my life.' What do you want the account of your life to say to the reader in summery? Your account must have a purpose, which is the central idea.

Write from memory.

An autobiography must be written from memory. You must not do research (interview individuals, read books, etc) to gather information for your account. It is ok to contact someone to be "reminded" of something such as the name of someone or the exact date that an event occurred. But you must not do a research to write your own life. Because you will write a firsthand account, you must write from your memory.

Structure your account.

You must decide on a sequence in which you will write your account. What will you write first, second, third, etc? This should not be difficult. You are about to write an autobiography, meaning that you will write your account in the very way your life has unfolded so far. To begin, you will need to structure your account as follows:

Early life

Start with your birth--when and where you were born, your parents and siblings--and your experiences as a child. You do not have to start with the common 'I was born in' line. But if this is the easiest way for you to begin, go ahead.

Teenage life

Disclose what you were like as a teenager, the schools you attended, your ambition (if any) at the time, hobbies, experiences with friends, and include anything or anyone who influenced you--directly or indirectly--the most.

Young adult life

Disclose things like college/ university attended, best friends and some experiences with them, happy or sad events that stand out in your mind, career choice, first job, how you met your spouse, hobbies at this time of your life, the birth of your first child (if any).

State what and how experiences have changed you in terms of how you think and act.

Remember that the readers are expecting you to grow. You need to show how you have grown from childhood, to teen, and to a young adult. To do this, give focus to the mature things that you did. Give details about your career.

The present

Disclose how experiences have shaped your mind over the years. What is your family or life like now? What do you do now?

The ending

Disclose what you think about your life looking back, and your achievements. Achievement does not have to be money or real estate. It may be, for example, long years of kindness.

Be truthful

Your autobiography must be the true account of your own life. It would be unwise to   embellish events of your life—or tell a lie—so as to create certain effect on the reader. You should stay true to your real life. One lie, if later exposed, might cast doubt on everything else in your account. So be truthful from beginning to end. If you know you cannot be truthful about a particular thing, it might be best to omit it.

When you are writing about an event that you have not personally witnessed—or of which you have no evidence—you must use preceding evidence like 'I think,' 'in my opinion,' or 'I was told by.' When any of these preceding phrases is used in front a piece of information, you make it clear to the reader that the information which follows is not firsthand. Thus you prevent the reader from assuming that you are lying.

Carefully consider before you reveal.

You have the liberty to choose what you will and will not reveal in your autobiography. It is your life. It is your account. Your autobiography may be your best means of   freeing yourself of dark secrets or painful emotions you have   been carrying for years. For example: a period of suicidal thoughts, childhood feelings of rejection; marital abuse. Only you can decide—with careful consideration—what events of your life will make it into your autobiography.

Relate the mood of each event in your account.

Your entire account should not be set on one mood. No one wants to read an autobiography that is entirely gloomy or happy. The reader wants to know the times when you were sad, frustrated, happy, disappointed, etc. Therefore you should relate each event the way you remember it.

Address any misconception of you.

Use your autobiography to clear away all significant misconceptions others might have of you. This is the account, in your own words, of your own life. Use it to clarify the kind of person you are. However, do not use your book to shoot philippics at others who have, or whom you assume have, done you wrong. Instead, clearly relate your side—or the correct side—of a conflict or   misunderstanding and allow the reader to make the final judgment.

Add photos to the account.

Add photos to the account to enliven it. As it is said, a photo tells a thousand words. Add photos of your childhood, of you at school, with family, etc.

What will make your autobiography sell?

If you want to make your autobiography a book, you most likely will want to sell copies of it hence the above question. If you are popular, your celebrity status answers the above question. Persons love to read more about celebrities. Many persons are interested in what famous persons (whether famous locally or internationally) do—such as their favourite foods, hobbies and what their life was like in the past, in the present; publicly and privately. So when a famous person decides to write an autobiography, his or her celebrity status answers the above question. Their autobiography will sell because of the public interest already in them.

If you are not famous (not a public figure or celebrity) the answer to the above question may not be simply answered because of who you are. When you are nobody (someone who is not of public interest or someone who the public does not readily recognize) your autobiography will not sell simply because you write about yourself.

So what will make your autobiography sell?

To make your autobiography satisfactorily sell, you may need to bring something to   the cover of your book that the public will recognize. In other words, your autobiography may need to carry the name of someone or something that will drag public interest. To help you understand, here is a test for you:

On this page are four cover titles of the same autobiography of John Doe. In this test you will be the public. As the public, you have not heard of nor seen John Doe before.   So which of the covers of John Doe's autobiography would most likely cause you   to purchase his book?

John Doe	I Am John Doe	John Doe My Life Story	John Doe The Life of a former Cannibal

You might say "but the public have many interests and how could I tell which would make the book sell?" True, the public have many interests—but the public have no interest in John Doe. The name John Doe (unlike the name Oprah Winfrey, for example) does not drag with it any public interest.

The best cover-title above, the title that should make the book satisfactorily sell, is:

John Doe
The Life of a
former
Cannibal

Why this cover title? This cover carries with it something that the public immediately recognizes—the word 'cannibal.' When a person sees the title of this book in a book store, or on a website, it is the word 'cannibal' (or the entire subtitle: *The life of a former cannibal*) that will make the person curious to read the book. The name John Doe is not immediately recognized with the public and therefore does not in and by itself attract public curiosity. It is the word 'cannibal' that creates the curiousity in the minds of many persons, hence causing them to make a purchase to read about John Doe.

This selling strategy also applies to the autobiography of a famous person. Adding an interest-catching subtitle to his or her autobiography will cause more copies of the book to sell.

While the public recognizes the name of a celebrity, an effectively written subtitle will cause more persons to buy. For example, an autobiography titled **Will Smith** will sell. But the same book with an interest-catching subtitle such as **Will Smith revealing what the public never knew** will do better.

The subtitle is a powerful tool. You must use it smartly, especially when an autobiography is about an unpopular or unknown subject. It should be written to drag interest to the book and thus increase sales. This means that the subtitle must carry with it—if the title fails to—something that the public will recognize and that will make them curious. So find something in your life's story—prison time, abortion, depression or something else that the public will have recognition with—to mention in the subtitle, or title, of your book.

Here are few subtitles that create a sense of curiousity. What is the word, or words, in the subtitle that drags your interest?

'From rags to riches'

'How I overcame depression'

'Why I never committed suicide'

'From a sinner to a winner'

Remember, your autobiography should carry a word or phrase in the subtitle that will prick the interest of the public to want to read.

Biography

A biography is an account of a person's life written by another person. But how does one write the account of another person's life? The truth is that every individual leaves footprints in the journey of his or her life. To write a biography of a person, you will have to trace the steps of that person to where his or her journey had begun.

Your task as biographer is to accurately narrate the life of the subject. Accuracy requires facts and truth. You may write a full biography or a partial biography.

Full biography

A full biography is an in-depth account of the life of the person (subject). It will carry major and minor details of the life of the person, typically resulting in a long book.

Partial biography

A partial biography only relates the major events in the life of the person and does not relate or detail many minor events.

Before you write a biography, you must first decide on whether it will be a full or partial account. Also, before you write, make sure you have a central idea of the person to write the account on. If it is the person who hires you to write the account, have a discussion on what the central idea will be. Ask the person this question: What is the main thought (s) you want readers to get from the biography?

It may be necessary to give yourself a deadline to complete the biography.

Getting down to action

So you have the subject for the biography, meaning you know whose life you will write about. You are now ready to write.

Here are your next steps as follows:

Research and write

To write a biography, you must commence a proper research on the subject. A proper research requires patience, dedication, and most likely a budget. You may have to make appointments, travel from place to place, and do long reading.

When carrying out your research, it is best to separate and investigate each area of the subject's life as follows:

Early life
Education
Career
Family life
Achievements
Death (if applicable)
Legacy

You will carry out your research by read literatures or articles on the subject, interview persons who personally knew the subject, interview the subject (if still alive or accessible) and just gather information from anything or anyone trust-worthy.

Structure your account in the following order:

1. Early life
2. Teenage and young adult life
3. Family life of the subject
4. Failures and Achievements (in business, personal life; career)
5. Legacy

You do not have to complete your research on the subject to begin to write. Once you have gathered a significant amount of information on the 'early life' of the subject, you should begin to write.

Do not narrow the biography on the subject.

You should not narrow every paragraph to the subject. You should broaden the information in your writing. For example: If the subject has served as a soldier in World War II, when you are writing about his time in the war, extend your writing to include when the war started, how it got started, and the countries which were involved. Yes, the book is about the subject. But the reader needs to also know a little about the things and persons who were important to a particular situation as the subject.

Add photos to the account

You should add photos of the subject to the biography. You may include photos of the subject, his family, the house in which he was born, tomb stone, etc. Photos of the subject—or photos of things appertain to the subject—will interest the reader.

How To Begin

When you sit down and begin to write, you must choose to write from the third person point of view. If you choose to write from the first person point of view, the biography will instead become a memoir. How so? The first person point of view puts the writer in the story as the 'I' character. The 'I' character would inevitably become another central character instead of only the person the account is about. In a biography, the focus must be on the person the account is about, not the writer. For this to happen, the account must be written from the third person point of view.

Memoir

A memoir is a historical account or biography written from the personal knowledge of the writer. The term 'personal knowledge' means knowledge gained firsthand. It is not knowledge the writer has gained through research. As a firsthand account, a memoir must be written entirely from memory. The first person point of view (the 'I" character) should be used.

A memoir must not be confused with an autobiography. When writing an autobiography, you are writing an account of your own life from birth to the present, and you are the subject of the account. But when you are writing a memoir, you are writing about someone else you personally knew or a <u>period of events</u> you have lived through. Though you are a part of the account, it is the period of events or person who is the subject of the account.

Biography

If your memoir is a biography, everything you write about the person must be from your personal experiences with such person. For example: If your memoir is about your deceased father (and let's say it is titled *Life with My Father*), then your account must be written from your personal experiences with your father. You will write about the things you did with him from childhood, lessons you have learnt from him, how his death affected you, things you observed of him as a father, husband, business man, etc. You will be writing your memories with your father. You should not dominate the account with information of your own life.

Importantly, a memoir is not about telling the life of the subject. It is really about <u>life with the subject</u>. Therefore you will begin the account by describing the first time you have met the subject or your earliest memories with the subject.

You may structure your account as follows:

Earliest memories:

Disclose your earliest memories with the subject, where and when. State how the relationship between the both of you got started. Describe the first effect the subject had on you.

Describe the subject:

From your own understanding, describe the subject. Is he (or she) smart, witty, business-minded, or something else? Describe the subject's background a little—where did he born, his education, etc. What are the subject's hobbies, likes, dislikes; career? Describe regular things you did together, major and minor.

Closing chapter:

Disclose what makes the subject special, giving the main impression you want readers to have of him. Disclose the most important thing or things you have learnt from the subject over the years. If the subject is deceased, disclose how the death of the subject has affected you. What is the main thing you will keep in your memory about him?

Historical account

If your memoir is a historical account, all the events in your account must be events which you have personally lived through. For example: If your memoir is about five years you have lived in captivity, the memoir must be about your experiences in the situation. Remember, it is the historical event that is the subject of the account—not you. So you must not make the mistake of writing about your life.   What you will write are your memories of the specific period of events. You will need to structure your account as shown below:

Start of the situation:

Disclose what led to you   been in the situation (prison, music industry, children home, or whatever it was) in the beginning.   The reader should get a pellucid insight into the beginning.

<u>Relate unfolded events:</u>

Disclose the things which happened while you were going into the situation—explaining what you saw, smelled, heard, did, felt, and was told.

If you are describing a situation in which you were too young to now remember the start, you must describe your earliest memories. You must describe your experiences in the situation until the end—the good and bad experiences—and persons you have met.

<u>The final chapter:</u>

Disclose how, why, and when you got out of the situation. Disclose what you have learnt from it, how it helped or affected you, and what you primarily want the reader to understand from your account. Disclose how you are now living your life.

Memoirs

This is a kind of autobiography that is typically written by a public figure—normally, a retired public figure. A public figure is someone in public service, such as a politician. (For the sake of no misunderstanding, memoirs and a memoir are different).

When writing your memoirs, you will write your firsthand experiences in public service and give some information of your personal life. You will structure your account as follows:

Beginning in public service

Relate in details how you got started in public service. Disclose what or who influenced you, directly or indirectly. Disclose the first significant meeting you had and with whom.

Early life

Give the reader little information on your life prior to public service. Disclose when and where you were born and to whom. Describe your parents (their careers, religion, personalities; rich or poor) and your siblings. Relate childhood experiences that you can recall.

Young adult life

Share to the reader what your life was like as a young adult—sharing things like college attended, sports team you played for, ambitions, etc.

Life in public service

Relate your experiences (good and bad) in public service. Relate—if applicable—how you have moved up the ladder. Relate important people you have met; important decisions you have made.

Personal life while a public figure

Disclose some things that went on in your personal life   while you were in public service—such as, for example,   divorce, depression, birth of a child; dating.

Closing on your public service experiences

If applicable, address any misconception others might have regarding any controversial decision you have made while in public service. Share your swan song.

Sum up your contributions.

Share your opinion on the present state of the public service you were part of. For example: If you were a long-serving police officer in Jamaica, what is your observation of the present state of the police force? If you were a politician, what is your observation of Jamaican politics now compared to your time in it?

Your life now

Disclose significant things you do now in retirement. Disclose what you think about your life looking back.

Recipe Book

In definition, a recipe is 'a list of ingredients and directions for doing something.' This means that a recipe has two parts: (a) ingredients and (b) instructions how to use such ingredients in composing something. In this section, you will be informed on how to put together a recipe book. The focus will be on food recipes.

What is a recipe book?

A recipe book is a book with a list of recipes. On first thought, a recipe book seems like a very simple book to publish. All I have to do, you might say, is to gather a list of recipes and publish them. But there are several bad things that might happen because of a poorly constructed recipe. For example, the reader might get diarrhea after trying out your food recipe. So like writing a biography, rules apply to writing and publishing a proper recipe book.

So what are the rules?

Know Each Recipe

Before you publish a recipe, ensure that the recipe works. You might be tempted to publish a recipe book using recipes you have gathered out of other books, from family members, or off the internet. But if you have not tested a recipe, you should not publish it in your book. Giving your readers an untested recipe is like a car manufacturer giving a buyer an untested car to drive. You might be putting the reader at risk!

You might ask: Do I have to test all 95 recipes for my book? The simple answer is 'yes.' To put a recipe through a test, you may either personally try it or watch   someone else (on YouTube, for example) execute it. The rule here is to ensure that a recipe works before selling it.

Be Precise

A recipe should be clearly and accurately   expressed to the reader. Avoid using vague terms like 'a little amount of butter' (Which type of butter?   How much butter is a little amount?), or 'half spoon of salt' (teaspoon or tablespoon?). The point is that if a recipe is not clear, it forces the reader to assume through the uncertainties which might cause the carrying out of the recipe to go wrong. So in your ingredients, be clear about portion (a tablespoon of cooking butter instead of 'a little amount of butter'). And write your direction showing:

How (example: <u>slowly</u> pour in milk),
When (example: apply icing <u>after</u> the cake cools)
Why (example: the icing will melt <u>if applied to the hot cake</u>).

<u>Not all recipe books are 'cook books'</u>

The term 'cook book' cannot be rightfully used on all recipe books. The term 'cook book' is only fitting for a book that contains recipes for cooking. For example, it would be incorrect to put the term 'cook book' on a book with recipes for baking.

<u>Specify optional elements</u>

You should let the reader know when something in the ingredients is optional. The reader might not know the things which are optional from the things which are required. Look at the piece of example below:

Ingredients
2 pounds flour
¼ pound cornmeal
Thyme (optional)
1 teaspoon baking powder

You should ensure that the things specified as 'optional' are not important to the outcome of what will be made. So how do you tell what is optional?

In many ingredients, there are the things which are part of the 'building' process and   the things which serve to simply 'enhance.'

For example: In the ingredients for a potato pudding, flour and potato build the pudding. So they are required. But the syrup for pouring on the finished pudding is optional. The pudding can be built and enjoyed without the use of syrup.

Suggest alternatives

Alternatives are useful for the reader, especially when an element of the ingredients might be difficult to obtain or a particular method might not be easy for everyone. Regarding ingredients, you may write—for example—*a teaspoon of vegetable oil or cooking butter*. The reader who does not have oil may use butter or the other way around. Regarding the direction, you may write—for example—*grater the cheese or cut it into fine slices*. The reader who does not have a grater will use the alternative.

So it is useful to give the reader an alternative. However, if the alternative instruction in the recipe is cumbersome or completely different, it would be better to write two versions of the recipe.

Stay to the recipe

Do not include something in the recipe that does not have anything to do with it. You might feel a strong desire to tell the reader how much the recipe means to you or how you and your husband love preparing it on a Sunday. Well, do not do this. A recipe must not include any distraction. A recipe should say to the reader 'here are the list of things you need to have and this is how you prepare them.'

If you want to tell the reader about your personal taste, interests, etc. do so in the introduction—not in the recipe itself.

Put mix recipes in order

If you will publish a book with mix recipes—example: recipes on baking, roasting, drinks, etc. instead of only on baking—it would be better to put the recipes in identified groups or chapters. For example, you put all baking recipes in chapter one, all drinks recipes in chapter two, etc. This will make your recipe book much easier for the reader to use.

You may also group recipes according to the time of day they represent. For example, breakfast recipes first, lunch recipes second, and dinner recipes close the book.

Target readers

What kind of interests are you targeting with your recipe book? You might reply right now by saying "I'm targeting anyone who cooks." Well, you are totally wrong to think that way.

People do not buy any recipe book—the same way people do not buy any car, any motorbike, or any biscuit in the supermarket. People do not buy a recipe book simply because it is a recipe book. They buy a recipe book because it offers recipes suited to their interests. So you should target specific interests with your book. For example: Are you writing a book with vegetarian recipes? If yes, you are targeting vegetarians. Are you writing a book with Jamaican recipes? If yes, you are targeting persons who want to learn how to prepare Jamaican dishes.

It is self-misleading to think that you can write a recipe book that will interest everyone.

So what is the benefit of targeting specific interests? The answer is simple: More people will buy your book. Every consumer has a key word or key words in mind when shopping. A shopper's key word for a recipe book might be 'organic food,' 'vegetables,' 'fish,' or something else. What key word or key words identify your book?

Another important thing is that the interest your book targets should be seen on the book cover. Look at this simple example above.

The images you put on the cover (today's recipe books do not look nice without at least one image or drawing on the cover) should represent the book correctly. It would be incorrect to put the image of fried chicken on the cover of a book with seafood recipes.

How To Write a Motivational Book

Motivational books are popular among readers. These books are written to make the readers keen to achieve something in the realities of their lives. Functionally, the purpose of a motivational book is to shape the minds of the readers by re-wiring their thoughts to ameliorate their actions. Therefore motivational books cover many of reality issues and problems—such as, for example, low self-esteem, loneliness, suicidal thoughts, career choices, stress, and stigma.

If you decide to write a motivational book, it is useful to do so using the following strategy:

Identify the problem: Your book must immediately identify what problem it is dealing with. The best place to start doing this is from the very cover of the book. If your book is on the subject of depression, this must be seen on the book cover—example: *'How to overcome depression.'* If you are dealing with depression only by a particular cause, this should be seen in the book tittle—example: *'How to handle depression during bankruptcy.'*

Define the problem: You must clearly define the problem your book is about before giving means of solution to the reader. Remember, some persons' problem is the problem of not understanding their problem. In other words, because they do not understand their problem, they have a problem. It is like trying to fix a car engine without first understanding what the problem of the engine is.

Let's say your book is about low self-esteem. Your first step is to define what low self-esteem is. The second step is to help the reader to acknowledge this problem in her life. The third step is to offer means of solution to the reader. Your job is now done, and it is now up to the reader to take action for a change in her life.

<u>Offer more than one solution:</u> More than one individual can have the same problem but their   different circumstances cause them to take different approaches to a solution. For example, many persons struggle with suicidal thoughts—some because of unemployment, some because of broken relationships, some because of penury, and others because of abuse. As you can see, these persons all suffer from the same problem but cannot be offered the same solution because of the different causes. Obviously, one cap does not fit all. So when giving means of solution, you should look at different causes of the problem. You will help more individuals this way.

Everyone needs motivation. Here are some additional things to consider if you choose to write a motivational book.

Choose a subject that excites you

Being a motivational writer (or speaker) does not mean that you can motivate others on everything. You do not know everything. So ensure that you choose a subject that you feel a burning desire to address.

First know what motivates you.

Before you motivate others, you must first know what motivates you. In other words, what is it that makes you want to motivate others on the particular subject you have chosen? Is it love, hate, anger, religion, politics; patriotism, etc.? To motivate others you first have to be pushed by something. So what is that 'something' that you are feeling inside you concerning your subject? Whatever it is, it should be positive as it will determine the quality and effects of your words.

Know who you want to target.

Who do you want to reach with your book? Are you targeting teens, married couples, black women, Christians, or some other group? You should have a <u>target audience</u> in mind before you write, even if the book will be suitable for anyone.

Be logical

What makes a successful motivational book (or a motivational speaker) is logical thinking. Without logics in what you write, you will fail terribly.

So think about every point that you want to write—from different angles—before you write. When you think from different angles, your effort must be to avoid being or sounding bias, unintelligent, or unknowledgeable. But bear in mind, though, that probably not everyone will agree with you on everything you write. You might be criticized, and that's ok.

Be Tactful

While motivational words must serve to spur and galvanize, you should ensure that your 'choice of words' are respectful of the opinions and rights of others. It is easy to lose tact when addressing situation you might consider frustrating (example, laziness) or immoral (example, homosexuality). The purpose of motivation is to bring about a change. If someone feels insulted or angered by what you write, he or she will not do what you say. So write tactfully.

Stay to the point

With every point that you make, it is wise to be precise and concise. You might find this a little difficult to do when you are writing a book, which is far more in length than a leaflet. You might want to lengthen your work by including experiences and examples. If you do, ensure that such experiences and examples you write serve to strengthen a point instead of straying away from it. You don't want to kill an important point with a long digression or extraneous statement.

Good luck!

How
To Self Publish
Your
Book

Offline & Online Publishing

Self publishing is the act of an author being the publisher of his own book. The author personally takes on the responsibility of taking his work from raw manuscript to a finished print and/or electronic book.

The self publisher may choose to publish his book offline or online. The finished book may be made available to consumers both online (e-book) and offline (physical copies). So what does it mean to publish your book online versus offline?

Offline Publishing

This is the method of book publishing which exists long before the advent of the internet. It is the process of preparing a manuscript into a book without the use of the internet. Therefore it is referred to as 'offline publishing.'

To publish your book offline, the first thing you need to have is a budget. You will need to have money to cover the expenses involved. To put your budget together, speak with different printers or book publishers that offer book printing services. Find the most suitable and cheapest one to use.

If you choose a printer (a printing business) to print and bind your book, ensure that they provide a barcode as part of their book printing service. This is because many book stores refuse to take a book that does not have a barcode.

If you choose a book publisher to print and bind your book, try to secure a deal with them to distribute copies of the book.   A book publisher (company that publishes books) might have its own distribution department. If not, the book publisher should be able to suggest a distributer you may use.

Whether you will use a printer or book publisher to print and bind your book, you will have the following onuses as a self-publisher:

1. *Manuscript Preparation*: Apart from the actual typing of the text, manuscript preparation at the publishing stage covers proofread, illustration, font size, colour, and text layout.

2. *Book size:* When contemplating the book size, make your decision base on the <u>genre of book</u> you will publish. Remember, any book size does not work well with any type of book. Go for a small book size when publishing a novel, handbook, self help, or poetry—just to name a few. Books in these genres are usually carried around (to the beach, on a bus, etc) by the reader and so the reader would not want a book that is big and cumbersome.

3. *Book Cover Design:* How your book looks affects how much attention it will get when it shows up in internet search results or when on a shelf in a book store. Appearance is very important. So never underestimate the power of appearance.

    When designing the cover of your book, what colour will it have and why that colour? Will you include image and why that image? Where will the title appear and how best can you make it look?

4. *ISBN Purchase:* The abbreviation ISBN stands for International Standard Book Number. This thirteen digits number (increased from ten to thirteen since January 1, 2007) must be on your book. If you are using a printer, they may provide this number as part of their services, otherwise you will have to buy it online or from an ISBN agent in your region. In Jamaica, an ISBN may be bought from the National Library of Jamaica.

5. *Marketing and Sales*: You may promote the finished book through words-of-mouth, internet (including YouTube; social media), a book launch, press, and radio/TV interviews. Try to

secure a distributor (s) to sell copies of the book.

Online Publishing

This is the method of book publishing   which uses the internet. Therefore it is referred to as 'online publishing.'   A book published via the internet is available to consumers either as an e-book (downloadable file) or as a physical copy (print on demand), or both. To publish your book online, you have the following option:

Sell your writing as a downloadable file: You may do this by making your book downloadable from your own website. Another way is to use a website that lets individuals sell digital items. Several websites are designed to let authors publish their writing as an electronic book (e-book). Two of such websites are Kdp.Amazon.com and Gumroad.com.

Kdp.Amazon.com

This website is part of Amazon and leads to its platform for individuals to self-publish e-books and paperbacks. The e-books are then downloadable to Amazon Kindles. Signing up is free and the process of setting up your book (s) is also free and very easy. You (the author) will choose to be paid through one of the following methods:

(a) To a bank account. You will add a bank account for receiving your royalties. (If you live outside the United States of America, you may live in a country not supported by this withdrawal method).

(b) By cheque. You may choose to receive your royalties by cheque. Amazon will send a cheque to you each time when your royalties reach at least $100 USD.

Gumroad.com

This website lets any individual self-publish e-books   and other digital items—such as pictures, audio books, and music. All you have to do is sign up for free, choose how you want to receive payments, and upload the manuscript file.

Once you have completed the uploading progress, you may start selling by sharing the Gumroad link for your e-book on your own website, in emails, and on social websites such as Facebook. You may withdraw your payments from Gumroad to a US bank account or PayPal account.

Understanding a book

There are three types of books—print book, e-book, and audio book.

A **print book** is defined as sheets of paper bound together inside a cover which exists either as a hardcover (the cover made of thick cardboard or leather) or a paperback (the cover made of thin paper).

An **e-book** is spelled out as an electronic book. It is a literature that is published electronically. The reader has to enjoy this book through the use of an electronic device—example: a tablet.

An **audio book** is an audible literature. A person enjoying this book is a listener, not a reader.

Each part of a book has a name. Here they are with their definition:

Cover: The paper or leather covering that wraps and protects the leaves of a book. Regarding e-book, the cover exists as an image on the website where it is marketed. Regarding audio book, the cover may exist as a website image and/or CD label. (The cover typically holds indentifying information about the book—such as the title, name of the author, ISBN, barcode, and a brief description of what the book is about).

Endpaper: This is a blank paper which is glued to the inner part of some book covers. (The use of an endpaper is normally to hide the raw inner look of a hardcover).

Flyleaf: This is a blank leaf of paper at the beginning or end of a book. (In some books, a flyleaf is at the beginning and another one is at the end).

Jacket (or Dust Cover): This is a loose paper covering for a book, either with promotional information or the same information as the cover.

Page: One side of a leaf in a book, magazine, etc. (This means that one leaf in a book carries two pages).

Spine: The left side of a closed book. It is the part of the book which faces outward when the book is properly shelved.

Contents of a Book

Acknowledgement: A statement by the author recognizing persons who have contributed in one way or the other to the writing of the book.

Addendum: Additional text added after the main text. (Example: a page about the author, a glossary, an epilogue, or an appendix).

Appendix: Supplementary text added after the main text. (An appendix is used to improve or update knowledge from the main text).

Bibliography: A list of the sources used in the preparation of the manuscript of a book.

Chapter: A section of a text that deals with a portion of what the text is about, identified by a heading with a number. Example: Part One or Chapter One.

Glossary: A list of words from the main text with their meanings. (A glossary is used when the main text contains jargons, technical terms, or uncommon words that the reader might not be fully familiar with).

Index: An alphabetical listing of names and topics along with page numbers where they are discussed.

Illustration: Pictures or drawing that depicts information in the book.

Main Text: The body of text dealing with what the book is about (distinct from introduction, glossary, footnote, etc).

Padding: Unnecessary text or images added to make a story or book longer.

Page number: (a) A particular number on a page in the numbering of all the pages in a book. Example: I know it is somewhere in the book but I don't remember the page number. (b) Pagination.

Preface: A short introductory essay that preludes the main text. (A preface may be used by the writer to impart the purpose of the book, what inspired the book, how to use the book, and/or what to expect in the book).

Types of Books

Types of books are first separated into two main categories, which are:

Fiction: Stories and other writings based on the imagination. (Genres under fiction include mystery, romance, and action-adventure).

Non-fiction: Stories and other writings based on the real world (Examples: biography, dictionary, and encyclopaedia).

A Moment with Literature

Through the changing of time, literature has been defined and redefined. Early definition of literature explains it as 'any written work.' As years went by, thoughts changed and there came the desire to see literature as something separate from just any written work. The formalistic definition holds literature as 'creative writing of recognized artistic or intellectual value.' For a work to be of artistic or intellectual value, it has to utilize language in ways that differ from ordinary use.

But the important thing is that both definition of literature stand. In the widest sense, literature is any single body of written work. In the formalistic sense, literature is 'creative writing of recognized artistic or intellectual value.' One definition does not override the other.

Literature points to words. Words constitute literature. Because there are different uses of words, literature has to be classified according to the different uses. *Oral literature* points to spoken stories, now including audio books. *Print literature* points to written fiction and non-fiction, and *electronic literature* points to fiction and non-fiction delivered electronically.

Literature is further classified according to the following:

Region: Caribbean literature, African literature, etc.
Language: German literature, Greek literature.
Religion: Islamic literature, Christian literature, etc.
Historical periods: Ancient Egyptian literature, West Indian literature, etc.

The purpose of literature

The purpose of literature is to pass on and preserve information, whether it is to educate or entertain.

The benefits of literature

People turn to literature for knowledge. Literature plays a crucial part in learning at any stage of life. Within literature lies knowledge of history, psychology, religious beliefs, medicine, and other areas of study. It keeps knowledge about many things from perishing. It was from early civilization that humans realized that in order for knowledge about themselves and what they know to survive, they must turn to literature. Without their dependence on literature, much medical, scientific, historical, and religious knowledge would get washed away with the passing of time. Take for example the Bible. No one today would know about Esther if someone had not written down her fascinating story. Jesus, or most of what is known about him, would have been forgotten had not Matthew, Mark, Luke, and John wrote literatures of his existence.

Literature is not only beneficial at the individual level but also on national and the international levels. At the individual level, though, the writer benefits through the satisfaction of relaying what is in his mind, whether it is imaginative or learned. There may also be monetary benefit too. Regular writing also sharpens the writer's self-expression and improves the quality of his literary output. For the reader, the benefit is being educated or entertained, or both.

Thanks for reading!

Nigel D. Salmon

ABOUT THE AUTHOR

Nigel D. Salmon is an author, literary speaker, book writing tutor and website designer. He is the founder of ninPol, his website design business, and the creator of JamaicaCitizensGuide.com. He lives in St Elizabeth, Jamaica.

Facebook: **Nigel D Salmon**

Instagram: **Nigel D Salmon**

Twitter: **Nigel D Salmon**

Website: **www.NigeldSalmon.com**

www.ingramcontent.com/pod-product-compliance
Lightning Source LLC
Chambersburg PA
CBHW060634290526
45793CB00001B/240